A VERY SHORT,
FAIRLY INTERESTING AND
REASONABLY CHEAP   BOOK ABOUT
KNOWLEDGE MANAGEMENT

A VERY SHORT,
FAIRLY INTERESTING AND
REASONABLY CHEAP BOOK ABOUT
KNOWLEDGE MANAGEMENT

JOANNE ROBERTS

SAGE

Los Angeles | London | New Delhi
Singapore | Washington DC | Boston

Los Angeles | London | New Delhi
Singapore | Washington DC | Boston

SAGE Publications Ltd
1 Oliver's Yard
55 City Road
London EC1Y 1SP

SAGE Publications Inc.
2455 Teller Road
Thousand Oaks, California 91320

SAGE Publications India Pvt Ltd
B 1/I 1 Mohan Cooperative Industrial Area
Mathura Road
New Delhi 110 044

SAGE Publications Asia-Pacific Pte Ltd
3 Church Street
#10-04 Samsung Hub
Singapore 049483

Editor: Kirst Smy
Editorial assistant: Molly Farrell
Production editor: Nicola Marshall
Copyeditor: Rose James
Proofreader: Sharon Cawood
Indexer: Silvia Benvenuto
Marketing manager: Catherine Slinn
Cover design: Wendy Scott
Typeset by: C&M Digitals (P) Ltd, Chennai, India
Printed in Great Britain by Henry Ling Limited at
The Dorset Press, Dorchester, DT1 1HD

The title for the 'Very Short, Fairly Interesting and
Reasonably Cheap Book about…Series' was devised
by Chris Grey. His book, *A Very Short, Fairly Interesting
and Reasonably Cheap Book about Studying
Organizations*, was the founding title of this series.

Chris Grey asserts his right to be recognized as
founding editor of the 'Very Short, Fairly Interesting and
Reasonably Cheap Book about...' series.

Library of Congress Control Number: 2014954834

British Library Cataloguing in Publication data

A catalogue record for this book is available from
the British Library

ISBN 978-0-8570-2246-2
ISBN 978-0-8570-2247-9 (pbk)

MIX
Paper from
responsible sources
FSC™ C013985

At SAGE we take sustainability seriously. Most of our products are printed in the UK using FSC papers and
boards. When we print overseas we ensure sustainable papers are used as measured by the Egmont grading
system. We undertake an annual audit to monitor our sustainability.

For John

Contents

List of Illustrations

Figures

Tables

Boxes

About the Author

Joanne Roberts is Professor in Arts and Cultural Management and director of the Winchester Luxury Research Group at Winchester School of Art, University of Southampton, UK. She has held posts in the business schools of Newcastle, Durham, and Northumbria Universities, UK. Her research interests include the internationalization of knowledge-intensive services, knowledge transfer, innovation and creativity, and critical perspectives on knowledge in organization and economy. She is currently investigating knowledge and ignorance in the field of luxury. Joanne is a member of several national and international scholarly networks, for example the Academy of International Business, the Critical Management Studies network, the British Academy of Management (BAM), and the Dynamics of Institutions and Markets in Europe (the DIME network of excellence). From 2009 to 2011 she chaired BAM's annual conference track on knowledge and learning.

Joanne has written extensively in the fields of business and management. She has published articles in a wide range of international journals, including the *Journal of Knowledge Management, Journal of Management Studies, Journal of Business Ethics, International Business Review, Management Learning, Research Policy,* and *The Service Industries Journal.* In addition, Joanne is author of *Multinational Business Services Firms* (Ashgate, 1998) and co-editor of three books: *Knowledge and Innovation in the New Service Economy,* with A. Andersen, J. Howells, R. Hull and I. Miles (Edward Elgar, 2000); *Living with Cyberspace,* with J. Armitage (Berg, 2002); and *Community, Economic Creativity and Organization,* with A. Amin (Oxford University Press, 2008). Joanne is also the co-founder and co-editor of the award-winning journal *Critical Perspectives on International Business*; an editor of the journal *Prometheus: Critical Studies in Innovation*; and member of the editorial board of several journals, including *Luxury: History, Culture and Consumption.* She is currently co-editing *Critical Luxury Studies: Art, Design, Media* with John Armitage for Edinburgh University Press.

Acknowledgements

The initial idea for this book was discussed with Delia Martinez Alfonso at the British Academy of Management Conference held in Brighton in 2009. I am grateful to her for seeing the book proposal through the review and commissioning stages. I am also grateful to the reviewers of the original proposal for their comments, which helped to shape the book. This project has had a rather long gestation period due to many distractions, and I must thank the team at Sage for their patience when successive deadlines were missed. In particular, Kirsty Smy's continued support has been vital to the realization of the project, as has the assistance of Nina Smith and Molly Farrell.

Many of the ideas developed in this book have benefited from presentation at conferences and workshops. Particular thanks go to participants in the Knowledge and Learning track of the British Academy of Management conferences from 2009 to 2011. I am also grateful for the helpful suggestions and comments of the reviewers of earlier drafts of the manuscript, which resulted in important improvements to the text. The book has of course benefited from the collective efforts of all those, past and present, engaged in research on knowledge in organization – to whom I am indebted.

I am grateful to Taylor & Francis Books for permission to reproduce a quote from Peter Drucker's (1993) *Post-Capitalist Society* (Oxford: Butterworth Heinemann). Additionally, I am indebted to Houghton Mifflin Harcourt for permission to reproduce in the USA the excerpt from 'Choruses from "The Rock"' from *The Complete Poems and Plays, 1909–1962* by T.S. Eliot (Orlando, FL: Harcourt, 1991) and to Faber and Faber Ltd for permission to reproduce the same excerpt from *The Complete Poems and Plays*, by T.S. Eliot (London: Faber and Faber, 1969) elsewhere in the world. My thanks also go to Manuela Tecusan for copyediting the text and for her translation of the quote from Diogenes Laertius.

Last but not least, my deepest thanks go to my partner, John Armitage, without whom this book and so much more would not be possible.

Should You Buy This Book?

This book, like others in the 'Very Short, Fairly Interesting and Reasonably Cheap Book about' series, conceived by Chris Grey, is designed mainly for university students – who in this case would be studying knowledge management as part of an undergraduate or post-graduate degree programme in the field of business and management, or else in computing studies, information management studies, or other related areas. This is not a textbook; it is much shorter, more interesting, and much cheaper than a standard text on knowledge management. What's more, it's a lot lighter: it can fit into your pocket and be read in a matter of hours rather than days (it's ideal for a long train journey or international flight).

The book might also appeal to academics who study in the field and would like to see a less conventional account of the knowledge management story. Moreover, academics from other disciplines who may wish to have a quick introduction to the field of knowledge management will find the book of value. Although it assumes a certain level of existing knowledge, this text is sufficiently accessible for the general reader keen to gain insight into knowledge management and an understanding of the implications of the shift towards a knowledge-based economy. Hence people who have encountered knowledge management in their workplace or through media reports and are curious to find out more about it will also profit from this book.

If you do buy this book and wish to take issue with anything you discover in its pages, or if you have experiences of knowledge management practices that can add to our understanding of the field and would like to share your knowledge, please get in touch. I would be delighted to hear from you, so please contact me at J.Roberts@soton.ac.uk

Introduction:

The Rise of Knowledge Management

Where is the Life we have lost in living?

Where is the wisdom we have lost in knowledge?

Where is the knowledge we have lost in information?

T. S. Eliot

The purpose of this book is to provide a short – but interesting and, importantly, critical – account of the rise of knowledge management and its current place in and implications for contemporary management theory and practice. To achieve this purpose it is necessary to explore where knowledge management comes from, what it is, why it is significant and where it is going. This will reveal the value of studying knowledge management in the global business environment. The book is not written solely for prospective or practicing managers – rather it is of relevance to everyone; for knowledge management is not something confined to large private or public sector organizations. Knowledge management of one sort or another is widespread. We are all touched by knowledge management systems of some description. From the Tesco supermarket checkout to hospital appointment systems, from the online booking of flights to the university or college admissions system, organizations collect information about us, analyse it, and use it to create knowledge about our purchasing habits, our travel preferences, our health, our qualifications – and much, much more.

Related to the idea of knowledge management is the popular debate on the knowledge economy, which, replete with associated concepts such as knowledge workers, knowing communities, and knowledge systems, pervades contemporary discussions of the competitiveness of organizations and of national and regional economies. The imperative to manage knowledge derives largely from the desire to improve competitiveness through innovation and through increased productivity, which in turn should arise from the creation and application of knowledge-based assets.

This introductory chapter focuses primarily on creating a context for later chapters by showing where knowledge management comes from. I begin with some initial observations on knowledge in general before exploring knowledge in the economy. I will then turn to knowledge in organizations and the rise of knowledge management. Then I will pause to elaborate a little on my motivation for writing this book before I proceed to a brief overview of the remaining chapters.

Knowledge: a few initial observations

The challenge of defining knowledge has given rise to a whole branch of philosophy that is concerned with it: epistemology – that is, the theory of knowledge. It would not be possible to explore this immense field in a short book – and the present one has a different purpose.[1] Nevertheless, a working definition of knowledge is required. According to the *Oxford Dictionary of English* (2003: 967), knowledge may be defined as 'facts, information, and skills acquired through experience or education; the theoretical or practical understanding of a subject ... the sum of what is known'. As this formulation indicates, there are several different types of knowledge, for example theoretical and practical. The varied nature of knowledge will be considered in the next chapter. For now, it is useful to begin our exploration of knowledge by drawing a clear distinction between data, information, and knowledge.

First, what is meant by the term 'data'? Data may be defined as series of observations, measurements, or facts – presented for example in the form of numbers, words, sounds, and/or images. Data have no meaning, but they provide the raw material from which information is produced. Information is defined as data that have been arranged into a meaningful pattern. Data may result from conducting a survey; information results from the analysis of these data in the form of a report, or of charts and graphs that give them meaning. Knowledge may be defined as the application and productive use of information. Knowledge is more than information, because it involves an awareness or an understanding gained through experience, familiarity, or learning. Yet the relationship between knowledge and information is symbiotic. Knowledge creation is dependent upon information, but the development of relevant information requires the application of knowledge. The tools and methods of analysis applied to information also influence knowledge creation. The same information can give rise to a variety of different types of knowledge, depending on the nature and purpose of the analysis.

To illustrate these differences between data, information, and knowledge, let's take a numerical example:

1 7 5 9 6 4 2 7 0 3 9 8 5 4

Here we have data in the form of a set of numbers. But what does the set mean? It could be a series of recorded observations – say, the number of times 10 individuals are able to catch a ball without dropping it:

17, 5, 9, 6, 4, 27, 0, 39, 8, 54

Combining this information with our existing knowledge, we can perhaps infer that those individuals with a higher number of catches have better hand–eye coordination than those with a lower number. Alternatively, by interpreting the numbers as one whole number, adding a dollar sign, and applying our knowledge of the USA's economy, we can take this set of numbers to represent the USA's outstanding public debt in July 2014 (TreasuryDirect, 2014):

$17,596,427,039,854

Imposing some form on the series of numbers transforms the raw data into information. Knowledge takes this process further. To produce knowledge from information, we need to combine this information with our existing understanding of the world, so that we can interpret the former and situate it in a context that gives it meaning.

The transformation of data into information and then into knowledge, as described above, illustrates a rationalist perspective on knowledge formation. Such a linear process may go beyond the stage where data constitute the raw material for information production and information provides the input for knowledge, to a stage where knowledge becomes the basis for 'wisdom' or 'meta-knowledge' – which includes beliefs and judgements (Figure 1.1). Importantly, wisdom recognizes the limits of knowledge and the uncertainties in the world (McKenna, 2005). Hence this is the point where our ignorance must be acknowledged.

In contrast to this linear representation, the relationship between data, information, knowledge, and wisdom (DIKW) is often represented in a hierarchical form, particularly among those concerned with the management of information. The exact origin of this representation is open to debate, and the DIKW hierarchy has been subject to much consideration and critique (see, for instance, Rowley, 2007, and Frické, 2009). Each tier of the hierarchy is thought to include all the categories below it (Figure 1.2).

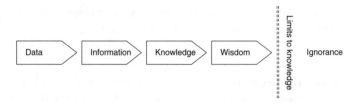

Figure 1.1   A linear process of knowledge formation and its limits

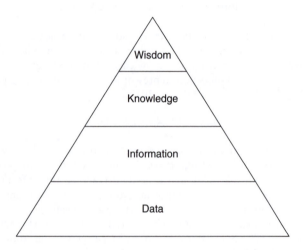

Figure 1.2   Data–information–knowledge–wisdom (DIKW) hierarchy

However, as noted above, the relationship between knowledge and information is symbiotic. Indeed the collection of data is also dependent on information and knowledge. Linear or hierarchical interpretations of the interactions between data, information, knowledge, and wisdom fail to employ wisdom in their construction. Acknowledging the full complexities of these interactions and transformations requires recognition that they may be multidirectional, recursive, and/or random. For instance, in the quotation at the beginning of this chapter, which comes from T. S. Eliot's Choruses in *The Rock* (Eliot, 1934), the poet and playwright suggests a reversal of the linear process of knowledge transformation outlined above.

In relation to our understanding of the knowledge we acquire from information, we must always be aware that our interpretation is dependent on our past experience and on our worldview. Moreover, in the western philosophical tradition knowledge tends to be defined as 'justified true belief'. For someone to have knowledge of something, that knowledge (or what is to count as such) must be true, and the person must not only believe it to be true but be justified in holding it – that is, their belief must be subject to empirical validation. But what counts as 'justified true belief' is open to question and very much dependent on the perspective from which we interpret empirical evidence. Such perspectives can change over time and in different contexts. Hence knowledge may be viewed as socially constructed.

For instance, before the heliocentric theory of the Renaissance astronomer Nicolaus Copernicus was accepted, it was commonly believed that the earth was the centre of the universe. Copernicus' theory, published just before his death in 1543, in *On the Revolutions of the Celestial Spheres*, contradicted accepted understandings of the position of the earth in the universe. Importantly, heliocentrism conflicted with the biblical account, which was of course supported by the powerful Roman Catholic church. Hence the dissemination of this new knowledge was impaired by the social and political structures of the time. Indeed in 1633 Galileo Galilei, the philosopher and astronomer credited with the introduction of significant improvements to the telescope, was tried by the Roman Inquisition for supporting heliocentrism. He was suspected of heresy and placed under house arrest for the remainder of his life.

This example illustrates two important points about knowledge. First, although we may believe that there are certain factual elements of knowledge that are true beyond doubt, we must remember that knowledge is socially constructed and dynamic in nature. Moreover, if we are wise, we will recognize, like the Greek philosopher Socrates, that our own ignorance is always vastly greater than our knowledge. Technological developments like the improved telescope in the early 1600s or the Internet in the twenty-first century can extend the scope of our knowledge; but they do not diminish our ignorance, since with new technologies come new unknowns. In addition, what is recognized as knowledge (or not) is highly contested. And this leads me to the second point: power influences what counts as – or is accepted as – real knowledge. In the seventeenth century the Roman Catholic church had the power to suppress knowledge that conflicted with its own dogma, according to which the earth was stationary and situated at the centre of the universe and the sun and stars rotated around it; and that dogma was accepted as real 'knowledge'.

The word 'knowledge' also possesses positive connotations. For example, who could disagree with the idea that knowledge is good, or that more knowledge is better than less? If knowledge is good, its accumulation and management must also be a good thing. It is this positive view of knowledge that permeates many business texts on knowledge management. Knowledge certainly does have a positive impact, as advances in medical knowledge over the past century demonstrate. Nonetheless, it is essential to recognize that there are negative aspects to it too. For instance, in recent years, major advances in knowledge of the human genome have provided a wide range of medical tests that can inform us about our predispositions to various life-threatening conditions; yet few of us wish to gain such knowledge. Perhaps sometimes ignorance is bliss. We might also question the value of knowledge of how to produce nuclear weapons, or the benefit of an excess of knowledge if it prevents timely decision making.

Hence knowledge is far from neutral; and, as I have already shown, what counts as knowledge is open to debate. The idea that 'knowledge is power', first articulated by the sixteenth-century English philosopher Francis Bacon, was later inverted into 'power is knowledge' by the twentieth-century French philosopher Michel Foucault (see Foucault, 1979). When considering knowledge, then, it is essential to recognize the power that access to it provides, as well as the way in which power itself can give legitimacy to knowledge claims. Moreover, as the philosopher and historian of science Thomas Kuhn noted, knowledge that reinforces or sits easily with our existing knowledge system is more readily accepted than one that requires a paradigm shift in our worldview (see Kuhn, 1996). Similarly, in societies dominated by rational modes of thinking, knowledge claims based on myth or faith will carry less weight than knowledge claims based on scientific reasoning. Clearly knowledge is complex, and through the pages of this book I will frequently return to the challenges and opportunities that such complexity presents for those who are seeking to manage it.

Knowledge in the economy

In today's world we are regularly bombarded with media messages telling us how important knowledge is; how we now live in a knowledge economy, where knowledge work is the primary occupation of most of the productive workforce. Nations, organizations, and individuals, we are told, must now live in a globally competitive knowledge environment. National and international organizations – for instance, the Work Foundation, the World Bank, the Organization for Economic Cooperation and Development (OECD) – regularly urge policymakers to develop knowledge resources though investments in education and in research and development (R&D). It is against this background of an increasing emphasis on knowledge in the economy that any study of knowledge management must be set.

We might ask: 'Why the sudden focus on knowledge? After all, hasn't knowledge always been important?' And, of course, we would be right. Knowledge has always been an important resource. From the earliest human societies until today, knowledge – be it awareness of the habitat and behaviour of prey in hunter-gatherer communities or our ability to contain infectious diseases in the advanced world – has been crucial to survival. As civilizations developed through specialization, trade, and agriculture, the types of knowledge that were available and relevant to the smooth functioning of society expanded and deepened. Methods of recording information in the form of counting devices became necessary. Early systems of writing, such as Egyptian hieroglyphs, emerged around 3000 BC; they were of the pictographic–ideographic variety (Figure 1.3). These forms of writing permitted the recording of a broad range of information, which supported the economic and political structures of the societies in which they developed. The Phoenicians' introduction, around 2000 BC, of alphabetic writing enabled the expression of any concept that can be formulated in language. The record-keeping requirements associated with the extensive trading activities of the Phoenicians very probably helped to stimulate this innovation: the documentation of knowledge has always been closely aligned to economic activity, whether to count sheep or to control and organize international trade.

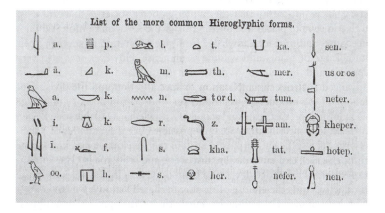

Figure 1.3 Common hieroglyphic forms

Source: *A Handbook for Travellers in Lower and Upper Egypt*. London: John Murray, Albemarle Street. Paris: Galignani; Boyveau. Malta: Critien; Watson. Cairo and Alexandria: V. Penasson. 1888. P. 069. Available from *Travelers in the Middle East Archive (TIMEA)*. Available at http://hdl.handle.net/1911/13077 (accessed 31 July 2014). This work is licensed under the Creative Commons Attribution 2.5 Generic License. To view a copy of this license, visit http://creativecommons.org/licenses/by/2.5/ or send a letter to Creative Commons, 444 Castro Street, Suite 900, Mountain View, California, 94041, USA.

These early means of recording information and preserving knowledge can be viewed as primitive or incipient knowledge management systems. Prior to their development, information and knowledge would have been passed on through oral traditions and through learning by doing. The central purpose of passing on knowledge – in writing or verbally, through explanation or through demonstration – is to ensure that the recipient does not spend time rediscovering it. And, of course, there is no guarantee that knowledge, once lost, can be easily restored. For instance, after the fall of the western part of the Roman Empire in the fifth century, Western Europe was plunged into a long period (often labelled the 'Dark Ages') during which much knowledge was lost – roughly until the Renaissance in the fourteenth century. Transferring knowledge can be more difficult than merely giving a verbal explanation or demonstration. I am sure that, like me, you have occasionally listened attentively to a lecture and yet failed to grasp what the professor seemed to be imparting in an eloquent and seemingly successful manner to other members of the audience. Knowledge transfer, let me repeat, is not a simple process. I will elaborate on this in Chapter 4.

The evolution and persistence of human civilization as we know it today depends on a vast accumulation of knowledge over several millennia and on the continued transfer of this knowledge from one generation to the next. Without the vast knowledge that the human race has stored and continues to gain, we would rapidly sink back into a primitive society. That is not to say that the hunter-gatherer societies that still exist today in remote places like the interior of the Amazon rainforest do not need, use, and transfer knowledge from one generation to another. Their knowledge of plants and wildlife is immense. However, it is also very specific and limited to a particular spatial and social context. In advanced societies the application of specialization and the division of labour in the production, reproduction, and distribution of knowledge account for the vast scale and scope of knowledge available today. Such division and specialization are only possible once the activities of a society produce sufficient surplus to sustain the development of knowledge through craft, experimentation, discovery, and scholarship. The application of new knowledge developed from these activities enables the more productive and efficient use of resources, thereby allowing us to enjoy a high level of material well-being. Furthermore, the application of appropriate knowledge can help us to optimize the use of limited material resources and to ensure their sustainability.

Clearly knowledge is important, and this has been recognized for several millennia. It has been preserved in ancient libraries (like the famous one constructed in Alexandria in Egypt by Alexander's successor Ptolemy Soter in the third century BC), revered by religious orders, protected and transferred through guilds, and – in Europe – taught and developed in universities since the eleventh century. More recently, knowledge has been collected, collated, analysed, and distributed on an unprecedented scale by global database providers. So why is there such an emphasis on knowledge and knowledge management at this point in time? Why has the spotlight fallen on this area in a way that is new? What is the difference between, say, knowledge in the nineteenth century and knowledge today? And why has knowledge become entangled in discussions of the economy in a way that was unknown until quite recently?

In the past, knowledge of production techniques, of resource availability, of market demand and supply conditions is what occupied centre stage. For instance, knowledge of crop rotation is vital to maintaining productive agriculture. Knowledge of identifying, efficiently extracting, and refining raw materials like oil, coal, and iron ore is central to industrialization. Knowledge of manufacturing methods, such as the float glass process for the mass production of glass, is vital for the manufacturing sector. Knowledge of market conditions ensures that products reach appropriate markets at the right time, in the required quantities, and in the best possible condition.

According to basic economic theory, there are four key resource endowments: capital, labour, land, and entrepreneurship. Until the late twentieth century, it was accepted wisdom that a country's economic wealth – and, by association, that of its people and organizations – came from combining these resources in the optimum fashion, given all other conditions. Consequently natural resource endowments, stocks of labour, capital, and entrepreneurial skills were central to competitiveness. But today natural resources derived from land are no longer a guarantee of competitiveness, since such resources can be acquired easily on global commodity markets. What is more, capital resources are now highly mobile, so they cannot be relied upon to secure a nation's competitiveness. Supplies of labour can no longer do that either, because low-skilled jobs – and, increasingly, high-skilled jobs too – can be offshored to low-cost locations in countries like India, Indonesia, Vietnam, and China. Today competitiveness is therefore embedded in highly skilled workforces, national endowments of entrepreneurial skills, as well as systems of knowledge; and these support and sustain competitive capacities in particular locations. At a national level, systems of knowledge and innovation creation and diffusion – which involve knowledge workers and appropriate institutional structures, from educational systems to regulatory and policy environments – are essential assets for nations that seek to secure economic competitiveness in the twenty-first century. The economist Chris Freeman described these systems as national systems of innovation in his seminal book *Technology Policy and Economic*

Performance: Lessons from Japan (Freeman, 1987). Building on his work, a substantial body of literature has developed that focuses on systems of innovation at national, regional, and sectoral levels. This literature is devoted to understanding the source of competitiveness in knowledge-based economies (see, for example, Lundvall, 1992; Edquist, 1997). Importantly, economic competitiveness is no longer determined by resource endowments, but rather by the ability to use such endowments to engage in innovation and creativity, in order to secure a proprietary claim over the most valuable, though often intangible, aspect of production. The competitiveness of firms is increasingly based on the ability to secure a profitable return on the intellectual property embodied in goods and services that may be produced and delivered by low-cost providers anywhere in the world.

Today, then, it is not knowledge so much as 'knowledge about knowledge' that has become a central economic resource. Indeed, the management guru Peter Drucker has argued that knowledge has become the only resource that can create a continuous competitive advantage for a firm or a nation (Drucker, 1993). Interestingly, Drucker was already exploring the changing nature of knowledge in the economy in the late 1950s, when he coined the phrase 'knowledge workers' for those whose work is primarily engaged in the creation, analysis, and application of knowledge and information (Drucker, 1969). Indeed analysis of knowledge in economy can be traced back to Alfred Marshall's (1890) study of the economies of agglomeration, which arose from the accumulation and circulation of skills and other knowledge resources in specific industrial districts in the late nineteenth century. Moreover, in 1945, Friedrich von Hayek elaborated on the use of knowledge in markets and in the economy. The phrase 'knowledge economy' originally emerged in 1962, in Fritz Machlup's *The Production and Distribution of Knowledge in the United States* (Machlup, 1962). This, together with other studies – including Daniel Bell's (1974) *The Coming of Post-Industrial Society* and Marc Porat's (1977) *Information Economy* – highlighted the growth of knowledge and information in the economic activity of the advanced economies and the dramatic rise in the value placed upon intellectual capital and intangible assets such as brands and intellectual property.

The knowledge economy

The economic historian Joel Mokyr (2002) traces the historical origins of the knowledge economy to the Enlightenment and to the Industrial Revolution that followed. The Enlightenment of eighteenth-century

Europe was a wide-ranging phenomenon that touched upon philosophical, social, cultural, and economic aspects of life. In terms of the development of knowledge, it marked an embrace of rational thinking, empiricism, and the use of the scientific method in combination with a secular approach to inquiry. Its relevance to the development of knowledge can be illustrated, in some senses, by the publication of the great French *Encyclopédie: Encyclopedia, or a Systematic Dictionary of the Sciences, Arts, and Crafts*. This general encyclopedia, edited by the French philosophers Denis Diderot and Jean le Rond d'Alembert and published in France between 1751 and 1772 in 17 volumes, was an attempt to provide a systematic record of human knowledge.

Over the past three centuries there has been a transformation not only in the amount of technical knowledge but also in its accessibility through publishing, universities, and professional networks. This improved access has brought about a continuous process of new-knowledge production and, subsequently, of sustained economic growth. Throughout the twentieth century social and technological developments intensified the use and the production of knowledge in economy and in society at large. At the beginning of the century the public provision of education became widespread in the rapidly industrializing nations, thereby increasing the knowledge capacities of their workforces. As the century progressed, the number of years that people spent in full-time education increased. Alongside this growth in the provision of education, technical advances – and most notably the development of the computer from the 1940s on – have transformed the capacity to collect, collate, analyse, create, and distribute new knowledge. In particular, the past three decades have seen improvements in our access to knowledge through the widespread application of information and communication technologies (ICTs) that facilitate the acceleration of new-knowledge production and the rate of technological change.

The notion of the 'knowledge economy' entered popular debate in the 1990s. It recognizes that the advanced economies derive a high proportion of their economic wealth from the creation, exploitation, and distribution of knowledge and information. In the past 20 years the role of knowledge in economic activity has received much attention from policymakers and management scholars. Yet there is no firm consensus on the definition of the knowledge economy. Indeed some even question whether such a phenomenon actually exists, or whether it is anything new. For instance, Smith (2002: 6) argues that the knowledge economy 'is at best a widely used metaphor, rather than a clear cut concept', while Roberts and Armitage (2008) question the validity of the notion by suggesting that the contemporary economy is characterized by ignorance as much as by knowledge. Godin (2006), for his part, suggests that the knowledge-based economy is simply a concept, promoted mainly by the OECD in order to direct the attention of policymakers to science and technology issues of relevance to the economy. Nevertheless, various efforts to define the knowledge economy have been made.

According to the OECD, knowledge economies are economies

> which are directly based on the production, distribution and use of knowledge and information. This is reflected in the trend in OECD economies towards growth in high-technology investments, high-technology industries, more highly skilled labour and associated productivity gains. (1996: 7)

Alternatively, Powell and Snellman define the knowledge economy as

> production and services based on knowledge-intensive activities that contribute to an accelerated pace of technological and scientific advance as well as equally rapid obsolescence. The key components of a knowledge economy include a greater reliance on intellectual capabilities than on physical inputs or natural resources, combined with efforts to integrate improvements in every stage of the production process, from the R&D lab to the factory floor to the interface with customers. (2004: 201)

Given such definitions, it is clear that a knowledge economy is very much a characteristic of advanced nations rather than a global phenomenon (Roberts, 2009).

When considering the knowledge economy, it is vital to recognize that knowledge is different from other commodities. Crucially, knowledge has a scarcity-defying quality. This arises from the public good nature of much knowledge. A public good is one that is non-rivalrous and non-excludable. The consumption of immaterial knowledge, information, ideas, and other abstract objects of thought is non-rivalrous in the sense that, if I share my knowledge with you, your gain does not diminish my stock of knowledge. Moreover, once new knowledge is shared and made public, it is difficult to exclude others from using it. The marginal, or extra, cost involved in acquiring it is virtually zero, because such knowledge is freely available and does not have to be rediscovered by each new consumer. Nevertheless, depending on the nature of the knowledge, the recipient may incur costs in order to develop the ability to understand and use it effectively. The public-good nature of much knowledge presents challenges for organizations that seek to profit from its development and exploitation. Securing a proprietary claim over knowledge can be difficult. If knowledge is publicly rather than privately owned, how can it be controlled and managed? We will return to the challenges arising from the nature of knowledge in Chapter 3.

From knowledge in organization to knowledge management

Alongside the growing recognition of the importance of knowledge in the economy, there has developed an awareness of knowledge in organizations. Organizing is about arranging, coordinating, or structuring resources to achieve a particular end. It is, then, about managing tangible and intangible resources with a view to achieving certain material or immaterial outputs. As organizations grow in size, the management and coordination of information and knowledge between their different parts become increasingly complex. In a sense, organizations are all about managing information and knowledge concerning inputs and outputs. Of course, since the rise of ICTs and the reduction in cost of telecommunications, we have seen some significant changes and developments in organizational forms, from hierarchical multidivisional organizations to flatter networks or virtual organizations. Nevertheless, fundamentally, the task of these organizational forms is to facilitate the effective management of information and knowledge so as to ensure the efficient operation of the organization.

Although, in the early twentieth century, organizations were concerned with using information and knowledge to facilitate the production of material goods, the importance of knowledge activities was already recognized. For example, in 1921 Frank Knight drew attention to the importance of knowledge activities in *Risk, Uncertainty and Profit* (Knight, 2010). Yet it was not until Edith Penrose (1959) put management control and development of knowledge resources at the heart of her *Theory of the Growth of the Firm* that the significance of knowledge as a resource – rather than as a means of managing other resources – gained recognition among economists and management theorists.

The ability to collect, collate, create, and distribute knowledge is now central to the competitiveness of many different kinds of organizations. In the 1980s and 1990s, the resource-based view (RBV) of the firm came to the fore in the field of strategic management; it was a view developed initially by Birger Wernerfelt (1984) and further elaborated upon by Jay Barney (1991) among others. This approach argues that the competitiveness of a firm is based on the application of the bundle of valuable resources at its disposal; and such resources include knowledge and information. Building on this, Robert M. Grant (1996) proposed the knowledge-based view (KBV) of the firm, arguing that knowledge is the firm's most strategically significant resource. Because knowledge-based resources are usually difficult to imitate, especially when they are embedded in organizational routines and practices, they can be a major source of sustained competitive advantage.

It is this turn towards a knowledge-based approach to understanding the resources of a firm, together with the growing emphasis on knowledge as a key source of competitiveness in national and regional economies, that has stimulated an interest in the active management of knowledge. Knowledge management includes 'any process or practice of creating, acquiring, capturing, sharing and using knowledge, wherever it resides, to enhance learning and performance in organizations' (Scarbrough, Swan, and Preston, 1999: 1). The adoption of knowledge management practices became widespread in the 1990s and, by the end of the decade, many large corporations and some smaller ones had appointed chief knowledge officers (Earl and Scott, 1999), signalling the central importance of knowledge to the organization. However, a number of corporations have since abandoned the role of chief knowledge officer, as they found that giving responsibility to one person absolved others of concern over the management of knowledge. Such developments have encouraged critics to argue that knowledge management is just another fad, along with other management fashions like total quality management, management by objectives, or business process re-engineering. I will return to the idea of knowledge management as a management fad in Chapter 7. For now, though, I want to say a few words about my own perspective before closing this chapter with a brief overview of the rest of the book.

Where I am coming from

As an academic studying organizations for over 20 years, I have observed with interest the transition of the leading economies from ones based on industries that produce tangible outputs to ones based on the production of intangible knowledge-based services – in other words, the transition from the industrial economy to the knowledge economy. This shift was typified in the UK by the decline of heavy industries like steel and shipbuilding in the 1980s and the rise of service industries, the burgeoning of the financial industries after deregulation in the 1980s, the emergence of call centres, the proliferation of retail parks, and, of course, the significant expansion of higher education since the early 1990s. Indeed my doctoral research was centrally concerned with this economic shift, focused as it was on the internationalization of knowledge-intensive business services such as advertising, accountancy, management consultancy, and computer service firms (Roberts, 1998). In the last three decades, ICTs have transformed production, distribution, and consumption activity, causing significant organizational change and new working practices. Alongside all these developments there has been an unprecedented process of globalization. With the liberalization of markets, the rising levels of international trade and investment, the increasing mobility of labour, and, of course, the rise of the Internet, knowledge and information can travel across the globe in an instant. All of these developments are intricately linked to the story of knowledge management.

I cannot elaborate in detail on all these changes in such a short book. Nevertheless, I can use them as a rich backdrop against which I will elucidate the rise of knowledge management and its key drivers and dimensions. In so doing, I will provide a critical appreciation of the foundations of knowledge management, the challenges of managing knowledge, and the key approaches adopted in knowledge management practices. From a management perspective, knowledge management appears as a technique to improve organizational performance. Nonetheless, its application, like that of any other management technique, can have a range of both positive and negative effects. My purpose in writing this book is to take a critical view of knowledge management. In the complex society in which we live, the management of knowledge, in one form or another, is essential. Nevertheless, I do want to question the theory and the practice of knowledge management. Indeed I want to challenge orthodox perspectives on the history, nature, and future of knowledge management. In this way I seek to offer an alternative to existing knowledge management texts. Moreover, through a critical engagement with extant research, I aim to provide readers with the means to question and evaluate contemporary knowledge management practices for themselves.

Importantly, I shall raise questions about what knowledge is created, captured, shared, and applied and for what purpose, for whose benefit, and at what cost. For instance, in relation to the drive to acquire and capture knowledge, I will question both the source of the knowledge acquired and the mechanisms through which it is captured. What, for example, are the implications of knowledge capture through the enforcement of intellectual property rights (IPRs) like patents and copyrights? Can improved organizational learning and performance be best achieved through the protection of proprietary knowledge? Or could an open approach to knowledge be more successful? Can a focus on knowledge lead to the neglect of other, equally significant aspects of management? Does knowledge management result in greater diversity of knowledge, or can it increase the tendency towards path dependency and the production of only a narrow range of knowledge? Today much of the most valuable organizational knowledge resides in the heads of employees. The challenges of managing such knowledge are significant. Is knowledge management a new strategy to manage knowledge workers? Or is it a sophisticated means of extracting knowledge from those same workers through a process of deskilling, as was elaborated by Harry Braverman (1974) in relation to workers in the 1960s and 1970s? Do knowledge management practices promote innovation and creativity, or do they prevent them? What are the limits of knowledge management? It is these and similar questions that I will raise throughout this book as I aim to provide readers with a fresh and innovative perspective on knowledge management.

How this book is organized

As this is a short book, I will not spend too much time elaborating on its contents here. Nevertheless, this final section will offer a very brief overview of what is to follow. Knowledge management is related to a number of academic and practitioner fields, namely organizational knowledge, organizational learning, and the learning organization. All of these fields are underpinned by the dependence of organizations on information. Chapter 2 will situate knowledge management within these competing, often overlapping, and yet complementary fields. This is followed in Chapter 3 by a reflection on whether knowledge can actually be managed. Here it is necessary to spend some time exploring different types of knowledge in order to assess the extent to which its various forms can be purposefully managed. Particular attention will be given to the distinction between explicit and tacit knowledge.

Following a broad overview of knowledge management, Chapter 4 will examine the central management issues concerning the acquisition, retention, and transfer of knowledge. These include efforts to capture and anchor knowledge within the organization – for instance, through IPRs and company-centred communities. The challenges of exchanging knowledge both within and beyond the boundaries of the organization will also be explored. Chapter 5 focuses on the importance of knowledge in the field of creativity and innovation. It begins by considering the nature of these two capacities; it outlines the challenge of organizing knowledge to support creativity and innovation; and it highlights the different organizational structures that are evident in various innovation contexts. This is followed by an examination of the knowledge-creating company and of the role of communities of practice as facilitators of creativity and innovation.

Chapter 6 explores issues related to knowledge management that are often given only scant attention in traditional knowledge management textbooks or are completely neglected, namely ignorance, forgetting, and unlearning. The high degree of specialization in the advanced economies ensures that, while individuals may be very knowledgeable in a certain field, they will also be deeply ignorant of many other areas. Yet ignorance, forgetting, and unlearning may offer opportunities for creativity, because existing knowledge might act as a barrier to new-knowledge development. This chapter will demonstrate the need to manage ignorance, forgetting, and unlearning alongside knowledge and learning.

The final chapter draws the book to a close by recognizing the limitations of such a very short volume even as it seeks to provide an interesting account of the dominant themes in knowledge management literature and practice. Diversity is rarely considered in the mainstream literature, and therefore a short reflection on its significance for knowledge management is provided. The chapter also offers some speculation on the future of knowledge management. Importantly, in this book I don't want to take for granted the positive connotations associated with knowledge. Rather I intend to take a critical stance on the value of knowledge management. The book will not provide a set of instructions on how to develop a knowledge management system; it will rather offer a set of questions that need to be asked of knowledge management practices. My aim is to offer you an appreciation of, and an ability to evaluate, the opportunities and challenges presented by knowledge management. I hope that, when you finish this book, you will have gained an understanding not only of what knowledge management is as a management technique, but also what it means for you as an individual, as a student, as an employee, as an entrepreneur, as a manager, as a consumer – and, above all, as a citizen.

Note

1. Suggested readings for those interested in exploring epistemology are provided in the Recommended Reading section of the Appendix.

2

Situating Knowledge Management

A place for everything, everything in its place.

Benjamin Franklin

Knowledge management is situated within a broader field of academic and practitioner interest in how organizations acquire and manage resources. In particular, the creation and acquisition of knowledge involve the managing of information and learning. Consequently, it makes sense to clarify here, at this early stage, how knowledge management is related to these other areas of academic and practitioner interest. By situating knowledge management within the broader study of organizations, it will be possible to identify its antecedents and to specify how it differs from and is related to the concepts of information management, organizational learning, the learning organization, and organizational knowledge.

The chapter begins by considering the place of information in the organization; then it goes on to explore the ideas of organizational learning and the learning organization. Next it outlines the emergence of organizational knowledge and knowledge management as academic and practitioner fields. Then it examines the relationship between knowledge and learning perspectives. The relevant areas of overlap between these academic and practitioner fields are then identified and examined; this will situate and clearly delineate the scope of knowledge management. The chapter concludes with an assessment of knowledge management as an academic field and management practice.

I begin, then, by exploring the relationship between information and organization.

Information and organization

Information is an essential element required in the organization of all living entities. Consider the complex organizations that occur in the insect world. Ants, for instance, live in colonies ranging in number and size from small to large – and the latter can have upwards of a million individuals, depending on the species. A division of labour operates within ant colonies such that work is allocated between various groups. Large colonies consist mostly of sterile wingless females who form castes of workers – nurses, soldiers, foragers or other specialized groups – such as a small number of fertile males called 'drones' and one or more fertile females called 'queens'. Ants are highly socialized insects. To coordinate their efforts, they communicate information through the exchange of pheromones – chemicals that trigger a social response in members of the same species. Moreover, they not only exchange information but are also active in collecting it. Worker ants outside the nest, such as scouts and patrollers, relay to foraging ants information about food sources or dangers by exchanging pheromones through physical contact or by leaving pheromone trails. Hence information and its dissemination and collection are of central significance to the form of organization that underpins the survival of ant colonies.

Information is equally important to the survival of humans, which is no less underpinned by the form of organization they live in. One of the features that distinguishes humans from other life forms is their sophisticated ability to communicate information across various media, most importantly through language. Using language, humans are able to share and develop complex abstract understandings of the world. The development of writing systems, some 5,000 years ago, permitted the externalization of such abstract appreciations of the world. This facilitated the spread of ideas across time and space and the extensive interrogation of, reflection upon, and combination and adaptation of concepts – as well as the development of theoretical constructs.

Information and its communication in the coordination of human interaction have been subject to much theoretical and practical investigation by information theorists and business and management scholars. Notable early contributions to theories of information include Norbert Wiener's (1948) *Cybernetics: Or Control and Communication in the Animal and the Machine*, and Claude Shannon and Warren Weaver's (1949) *The Mathematical Theory of Communication*.[1] Moreover, as many scholars like the Nobel prize-winning economists Ronald Coase (1937) and Friedrich von Hayek (1945) have shown, comprehending the role of information is fundamental to understanding the economics of organizations and markets. In his seminal article on 'The nature of the firm', for instance, Coase (1937) attributes the existence of firms to transaction costs, which include the costs of information and search.

The management of information has occurred ever since people began to keep records of activities and, as noted in Chapter 1, recording often arose from a need to keep track of commercial activities. In short, information management entails acquiring, maintaining, organizing, and retrieving information in various forms, from paper files to electronic-based digital records. A library, for example, represents a form of information management system, as does a Rolodex rotating file device or a digital personal organizer used for storing business contact details. Similarly, the activities of governance, whether economic or political, create a need for information management in the form of the construction and maintenance of records – for instance, concerning accounts of stocks, sales, debts, profits, tax revenues and collections, population census data, and land registration. The need for such activities gives rise to bureaucracy, that is, to an administrative system that is responsible for the management of information and resources according to predetermined rules and procedures. As economies develop, governance activities become increasingly complex and information management becomes a widespread necessity.

An early example of an information management exercise is the survey commissioned by William the Conqueror in 1086 to assess the land and the resources owned in England with the purpose of determining the amount of tax that could be raised. The comprehensive scale of the process and the irreversible nature of the information collected led people to compare the survey to the Last Judgement; hence it became known as *The Domesday Book*.[2] This negative view of the collection process reflected people's concerns about the nature of the information collected, the use to which it would be put, and its accuracy. Such concerns are equally relevant today. For example, an incorrect entry on our financial records can result in a poor credit rating and therefore in difficulty securing a mortgage.

In today's world the management of information is not confined to the bureaucracies of government and business. We all engage in it: we manage growing amounts of personal information concerning our own lives and interactions with family, friends, and actual and prospective employers. The paper-based diary, the address book, and the curriculum vitae as personal information management systems have given way to the ubiquitous computing embedded in mobile telephones, tablets, Internet-based personal blogs, or social and professional networking sites like Facebook and LinkedIn. Our personal information is no longer stored in tangible objects that we possess, but rather in cyberspace, where it is accessible through the Internet and cloud computing. Combined with the rise of web-based recreational activities, the development of digital personal information management systems embedded in mobile telephones, with their ability to interface with social and workplace networks and multimedia digital recording devices, has resulted in an upsurge in personal information management activity. While online data storage facilities may seem ephemeral to their users, in fact tangible resources facilitate them. The Internet allows for the centralization of data storage in huge computer server farms, such as the one owned by Google in the town of The Dalles, Oregon, USA, which is two stories high and approximately the size of two football fields (Markoff and Hansell, 2006).

The task of organizing is itself all about managing information. Organizing involves making decisions on the basis of the available information. As James G. March and Herbert A. Simon note:

> Organizations are systems of coordinated action among individuals and groups whose preferences, information, interests, or knowledge differ. Organization theories describe the delicate conversion of conflict into cooperation, the mobilization of resources, and the coordination of effort that facilitate the joint survival of an organization and its members. ... These contributions to survival are accomplished primarily through control over information, identities, stories, and incentives. *Organizations process and channel information.* (1993: 2; emphasis added)

The management of information, then, lies at the heart of the organization. When organizations are small, simple organizational structures – like a peer group or a simple hierarchy – can facilitate the efficient management and communication of information through direct interactions between members. Nevertheless, decision making is more time-consuming in a peer group, as all members may be involved in evaluating the information upon which the decision is made, whereas in a simple hierarchy

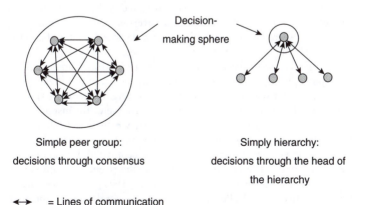

Decision-making sphere

Simple peer group:
decisions through consensus

Simply hierarchy:
decisions through the head of
the hierarchy

←→   = Lines of communication

Figure 2.1   The communication of information and decision making: simple peer group versus simple hierarchy

only the head needs to hold and analyse all the relevant information to make a decision. The main lines of communication in these two competing organizational forms are shown in Figure 2.1. Clearly the need for members of a peer group to develop a consensus on decisions requires a greater flow of communication than when one individual is given responsibility for decision making.

However, as organizations grow in complexity, so too does the challenge of information management. The efficient collection, collation, and analysis of information upon which decisions are based may require the development of complex hierarchical management structures. Moreover, as organizations develop, uncertainties and complexity increase, with implications for decision-making processes. It is important to recognize that an individual's decision-making capacity is subject to what Herbert Simon (1955) referred to as 'bounded rationality'. From a neoclassical economic perspective, individuals are thought to act rationally. Yet Simon highlighted the challenges they face because their ability to make rational decisions is limited – and limited not only by the ability to access all the relevant information, but also by the finite cognitive capacities available to humans for processing information within a specific timescale. Hence an individual's rationality is bounded. To some extent, the development of organizations and hierarchical structures allows for specialization in decision making, thereby overcoming some of the limitations of the bounded rationality of individuals. Nevertheless, organizations are also subject to cognitive limitations in terms of the availability of managerial attention (Simon, 1973). The management of an organization may be ignorant of the activities of the organization's members; perhaps this is due to the highly specialized knowledge required in the performance of a particular role, or to lack of managerial oversight, to managerial negligence, or to secretive or deceitful activities deployed by specific actors within or beyond the organization's boundaries.

An organization's structure adapts over time, to accommodate the developing priorities of its stakeholders as well as to address weaknesses in current decision-making processes. Organizational structures also respond to changes in the external environment; for instance, they responded to the growth of mass markets, which was facilitated by developments in transportation and communication technologies that unified national markets in the nineteenth century and promoted the rise of international and global markets in the twentieth century. The economic historian Alfred D. Chandler (1962, 1977) traced how organizations as diverse as Du Pont, Standard Oil, General Motors, and Sears Roebuck & Co. embraced the opportunities and challenges of the external environment by engaging in large-scale production and thereby achieving economies of scale in the use of expensive investments in locationally concentrated tangible assets. In so doing, these organizations developed increasingly sophisticated hierarchical structures designed to manage and channel the expanding flows of information associated with mass production and distribution.

The application of managerial techniques – including Taylorist and Fordist production systems – from the early twentieth century on increased the efficiency of production but simultaneously extended the information requirements of organizations. As large-scale organizations expanded in order to diversify their outputs as well as to serve mass markets at home and abroad, their organizational structures evolved: from unitary or functional structures organized around specialist functions like sales, manufacturing, and research and development, they became multidivisional hierarchical structures, organized around product and/or geographical divisions.

Such modern organizations came to dominate the economic landscape of the industrialized world for a large part of the twentieth century. Yet, by the 1970s, these huge, often vertically integrated organizations became increasingly vulnerable, confronted as they were with competition from producers in Japan and in the newly industrialized countries of the Far East. Additionally, western organizations in particular were facing oil price rises, economic recession, and stagflation, all of which contributed to a shift away from demand management to market-led neoliberal economic policies. These macroeconomic shocks encouraged the emergence of new organizational forms in the 1970s, which have been referred to as post-Fordist or postmodern organizations because they reflect a move away from the modern Fordist systems characterized by mass standardized production towards more flexible systems (Amin, 1994).

Western businesses were also influenced by the success of their Japanese competitors, which was based on management practices such as 'just in time' production, continuous improvement, and quality circles. Through the adoption of 'flexible specialization', organizations began to produce customized goods and services in an efficient and timely fashion. In addition, through the process of downsizing, restructuring, and outsourcing of non-core activities, they gained greater flexibility, which was reflected in their ability to adapt to changing market conditions. However, such flexibility increased the challenges of coordinating organizational activities – with important consequences for the management of information. Hence information and communication technologies (ICTs), which had become widely available by the 1980s, were key facilitators of these organizational developments because they enabled the coordination of flexible production systems within and between organizations across space and time.

In addition, by the end of the twentieth century the key sources of competitiveness for organizations had migrated from access to large-scale capital-intensive production systems to knowledge and information. The ability to adapt flexibly to market opportunities suddenly depended not on vast amounts of capital equipment, but on knowing how to access such assets in an efficient and cost-effective manner. The rise of the so-called postmodern organization is reflected in the relative decline of large, vertically integrated organizations and the development of what Castells (1996) describes as the 'networked enterprise'; examples include Dell, the computer supplier, and Cisco Systems, the provider of Internet equipment.

Despite changes in the scale and structure of organizations, information management remains at their heart, whether they are large or small, local or global. In the contemporary era ICTs allow for information to be gathered, collated, and analysed with increasing rapidity and on an expanding spatial scale. Indeed, in some instances, information technology management has come to dominate information management. First, the emergence of computers and communication technologies, then the advent of digital convergence have extended the scope for the collection and management of information. Indeed the expressions 'information management' and 'knowledge management' are often used interchangeably. The extent to which a distinction can be drawn between the two really depends on what we mean by knowledge; but this is something we will return to in Chapter 3. Information management as a field of study precedes knowledge management, as does the field of organizational learning, to which our attention now turns.

Organizational learning and the learning organization

If information is central to the functioning of organizations, the question of how it is acquired and distributed within them arises. The acquisition, production, and transfer of information and knowledge may be conceptualized in terms of learning. This learning perspective has given rise to a body of management literature that deals with organizational learning and the learning organization. The antecedents of organizational learning can be traced to studies of the organization as an information-processing system during the 1950s (Mirvis, 1996). In 1958, for instance, March and Simon's (1993) organizational theory identified a search for new information with the need to understand underperformance and to develop corrective action. Through a process of search and adaptation, successful organizations learn to develop efficient data-processing and decision-making systems and thereby improve their performance.

The notion of organizational learning was originally developed in Richard M. Cyert and James G. March's (1963) *A Behavioral Theory of the Firm*, as part of the authors' model of decision making within the firm. Over time, organizations learn; this is a necessary response to changes in the external environment. Organizations must adapt to survive. Responses to short-run feedback from the environment are determined by fairly well-defined rules. These rules evolve in response to longer-run feedback, according to some more general rules (Cyert and March, 1963: 101–2).

Such ideas about organizational learning as a means of adapting to the environment and as a result of experience have been taken up in the field of organizational learning. Thus Vincent E. Cangelosi and William R. Dill (1965), in the first publication that included organizational learning in its title ('Organizational learning: observations towards a theory'), critiqued the work of Cyert and March. They argued that it was only appropriate for organizations in stable environments, and they offered a model of organizational learning that acknowledged the tensions between individual and organizational levels of learning.

Chris Argyris and Donald Schön's (1978) book *Organizational Learning: A Theory of Action Perspective* proved to be a seminal contribution to the field. The work is perhaps best known for the development of the distinction between single-loop and double-loop learning. Single-looped learning occurs when organizational errors are detected and corrected, allowing the organization to proceed with its present policies to achieve its current objectives. Double-loop learning takes place when the correction of an organizational error requires the modification of the organization's underlying norms, policies, and objectives. Argyris and Schön also identify deutero-learning, which involves inquiry into the organization's own learning system. Using established learning theories, Argyris and Schön developed a new approach to organizational learning, which recognized that the individual is an agent of organizational learning: it is through individual learning that organizational structure, values, norms, and abilities evolve, in response to the changing internal and external environment. Argyris and Schön also drew a distinction between organizations with and organizations without the capacity to engage in significant learning. Importantly, they note that contrary to the view that underpins economic approaches to understanding organizations, human behaviour in organizations does not often conform to what is expected of a rational economic actor. Moreover, institutional rigidities – whether formal, like rules and procedures, or informal, like norms and values – can present barriers to learning.

Although originating in the 1950s, organizational learning did not became popular in the field of management studies until the 1980s, when important contributions were made by Hedberg (1981), Shrivastra (1983), Draft and Weick (1984), and Fiol and Lyles (1985). The publication in 1991 of a special issue of the journal *Organization Science* that was dedicated to organizational learning and gathered the now highly cited papers by March (1991), Huber (1991), Epple, Argote, and Devadas (1991), and Simon (1991) (among others), contributed to the popularization of the field.

The related idea of the learning organization emerged in the late 1980s. Bob Garrat's *The Learning Organization* was published in 1987 and the next year Robert Hayes, Steven Wheelwright, and Kim Clark published *Dynamic Manufacturing: Creating the Learning Organization* (see Garrat, 1987; Hayes et al., 1988). Yet the concept did not attract significant attention until the publication of Peter Senge's *The Fifth Discipline: The Art and Practice of the Learning Organization*, which became a key source for academics and practitioners alike. This book defines a learning organization as 'a place where people continually expand their capacity of creating results they really want, where patterns of thinking are broadened and nurtured, where collective aspiration is free and where people continually learn to learn' (Senge, 1990: 1).

The literature on the learning organization remains more limited than that on organizational learning. This may be partly accounted for by the less enthusiastic reception of the idea among North American scholars than among European ones (Easterby-Smith and Lyles, 2005). Besides, the learning organization literature is more prescriptive in nature, because it is concerned with how an organization should learn; it is therefore more practice-oriented. In contrast, organizational learning is chiefly concerned with describing and theorizing how organizations learn (Vera and Crossan, 2005). Hence the proportion of academic to total publications concerned with the learning organization is lower than the proportion of academic to total publications devoted to organizational learning – a fact that reflects just this difference (Table 2.1). As we will see in the next section, this difference in scholarly attention between a descriptive and prescriptive perspective is also evident when we compare the fields of organizational knowledge and knowledge management.

Organizational knowledge and knowledge management

The concept of organizational knowledge can be used in a general sense, to refer to knowledge about the organization – that is, about the various activities and actors that comprise it. In this use, the concept belongs to the vast body of management knowledge that has accumulated since the emergence of management as a discipline in the early twentieth century. Here, though, the focus is on knowledge as a resource within the organization, in line with Grant's (1996) knowledge-based view (KBV) of the firm. Organizational knowledge thus refers to knowledge embedded in the organization's assets – databases, intellectual property rights (IPRs), routines, processes, practices, and norms – as well as in the organization's members, both as individuals and as communities. Significantly, then, organizational knowledge includes knowledge embedded in the

Table 2.1 Publications concerning organizational learning, learning organization, organizational knowledge and knowledge management

Range of search	All publications		Academic journal publications		Academic journal publications as percentage of all publications
Search term*	Number	Date of earliest publication	Number	Date of earliest publication	
Organizational learning	866	1965	769	1965	88.80
Learning organization	342	1988	215	1992	62.87
Organizational knowledge	138	1992	110	1992	79.71
Knowledge Management	1851	1974	1211	1974	65.42

Notes: * Searches included English and American spellings of the terms.

Source: Compiled from data available from EBSCO Business Premier Database on 2 August 2012. Boolean searches of the terms in publication titles. *Business Source Premier*, the industry's most popular business research database, features the full text for more than 2,100 journals. Full text is provided back to 1965, and searchable cited references back to 1998 (http://www.ebscohost.com/academic/business-source-premier).

organization's assets and actions. Here studying organizational knowledge places a focus on how an organization's members, individually and collectively, use forms of knowledge to carry out their tasks and to develop new products and new ways of accomplishing their work.

The study of knowledge in organizations has attracted academic interest since the early twentieth century, primarily in the field of economics. For instance, in his seminal article 'The use of knowledge in society', the economist Friedrich von Hayek (1945) focused on the problem of how knowledge dispersed among individuals is coordinated such that it may be used to make decisions for organizations and society. For Hayek, the key coordinating mechanism through which knowledge is organized in society is the price mechanism. Markets bring together distributed knowledge related to a particular commodity or service and reflect this knowledge in the equilibrium market price. Importantly, Hayek emphasized the significance of unorganized knowledge:

> It is with respect to this that practically every individual has some advantage over all others in that he possesses unique information of which beneficial use might be made, but of which use can be made only if the decisions depending on it are left to him or are made with his active cooperation. We need to remember only how much we have to learn in any occupation after we have completed our theoretical training, how big a part of our working life we spend learning particular jobs, and how valuable an asset in all walks of life is knowledge of people, of local conditions, and special circumstances. … the shipper who earns his living from using otherwise empty or half-filled tramp-steamers, or the estate agent whose whole knowledge is almost exclusively one of temporary opportunities, or the *arbitrageur* who gains from local differences of commodity prices, are all performing eminently useful functions based on special knowledge of circumstances of the fleeting moment not known to others. (1945: 521–2)

Hayek critiques the idea of central planning by arguing that, while policymakers and economic planners may have access to knowledge embedded in aggregate data, they lack the detailed situational knowledge from which such data are drawn. Moreover, the rapidity with which circumstances evolve, even in periods of relative stability, results in aggregate data failing to capture knowledge of current situations. In contrast, market prices adapt speedily to new knowledge.

While Hayek's contribution has relevance for organizations, his concerns were focused predominantly at a societal level. In contrast, Edith Penrose's (1959) *Theory of the Growth of the Firm* focused on knowledge within the firm, in particular on knowledge embedded in resources, and further still in human resources. Penrose refers to the knowledge of managers, which develops through collective experience, and she attributes the rate of growth of firms to the availability of managerial resources dedicated to facilitating the process of expansion. Her work provided an essential foundation for the development of the resource-based view of the firm (Wernerfelt, 1984; Barney, 1991) and for the subsequent development of the knowledge-based view of the firm (Grant, 1996).

Around the time Penrose was exploring knowledge in organizations, the American Nobel prize-winning economist Kenneth Arrow was paying heed to learning and knowledge creation and diffusion within organizations and society (see Arrow, 1962, 1969), and the sociologist Everett Rogers was investigating the diffusion of new knowledge through society – with research published in his landmark text on the *Diffusion of Innovations* (Rogers, 1962). This interest in the management of knowledge at a societal level was very much in line with contemporary contributions to the idea of the knowledge (or information) economy (or society) (Machlup, 1962; Drucker, 1969).

In the early 1980s Richard Nelson and Sydney Winter argued that much of the organization's knowledge is embedded in its practices, in the form of routines and operating procedures: 'the routinization of activity in an organization constitutes the most important form of storage of the organization's specific operational knowledge' (1982: 99). For these authors, routines are repositories of an organization's memory and their influence on the evolution of firms is analogous to the role of genes in biological evolution. From this perspective, knowledge is the result of endogenous and historical learning processes through which routines and procedures develop; and these in turn influence the future evolution of organizational capacities and behaviour. In this sense, organizational knowledge can be considered to be distinct from the knowledge embedded in the individual members of an organization.

Early academic contributions to understanding knowledge management focused largely on the public and non-profit sectors (Wilensky, 1967; Carroll and Henry, 1975). Caldwell (1967), for example, was concerned with the management of scientific and technical knowledge from a public policy perspective. Knowledge management as a practice can be traced back to 1975, when Chaparral Steel adopted an organizational structure and a corporate strategy designed to rely directly on the explicit management of knowledge without the assistance of information technology (Wiig, 1997). By the end of the 1980s, knowledge management was growing in popularity in practitioner circles. Yet it was not until the 1990s that knowledge management attracted significant attention from management scholars and the concept entered popular management discourse.

The widespread uptake of knowledge management as a topic of academic interest can be in part attributed to a number of influential texts published in the mid- to late 1990s: Ikujiro Nonaka and Hirotaka Takeuchi's (1995) *The Knowledge-Creating Company*; Dorothy Leonard-Barton's (1995) *Wellsprings of Knowledge*; Thomas Davenport and Laurence Prusak's (1998) *Working Knowledge*; and Max Boisot's (1998) *Knowledge Assets*. The issues discussed in these books covered much the same ground as in earlier decades, but these more recent works are commonly identified as the original source of the academic field of knowledge management.

How the practice of knowledge management became popular in the late 1980s and early 1990s may explain why its academic heritage has been overlooked in the management literature. Consultants and information technology (IT) played a significant role. Knowledge is a core asset for consultancy companies; as a result, they were among the first organizations to invest in the management of knowledge, and in particular in the use of IT to capture and disseminate knowledge. Consequently, Koenig and Neveroski (2008) place the source of current-day knowledge management squarely at the door of consultancy firms, arguing that, as these firms developed expertise in the management of their own geographically dispersed knowledge-based organizations, they realized that they could market this expertise to other organizations. Hence, for most organizations, the internal evolution of knowledge management was overtaken by the external development of commercially available knowledge management tools and practices promoted by external suppliers.

Moreover, the promotion of knowledge management was also driven by the increasing availability of technologies designed to manage information. While consultants were eager to promote their services, IT hardware and software producers were equally keen to encourage sales of their knowledge management products. Additionally, the falling relative cost of computer and networking capacities since the early 1990s facilitated the widespread proliferation of company-wide computer networks and the adoption of software such as Lotus Notes® and Microsoft® Exchange Server to promote the efficient management of information and knowledge within and between organizations. Hence the practice of knowledge management was initially advanced in the form of IT systems designed to leverage knowledge and information as resources within companies. However, the limitation of knowledge management in the form of information management systems became apparent to academics and practitioners, who noted these systems' neglect of aspects related to people (Davenport, De Long, and Beers, 1998; Hull, 2000). In response, knowledge management practices have extended to incorporate the social elements, for example through the introduction of knowledge communities.

In parallel to the adoption and spread of knowledge management as a practice since the mid-1990s, there has been a rapid expansion of scholarly interest in the field, as evidenced in the growing number of articles on the topic (see Table 2.1). Moreover, to facilitate the dissemination of academic knowledge, a number of journals have been launched since the late 1990s – for instance, the *Journal of Knowledge Management*, *Knowledge and Process Management*; *Knowledge Management Research & Practice*; and the *International Journal of Knowledge Management* (see Appendix).

Knowledge and learning in organizations: competing or converging fields?

Effective organizational learning and knowledge management are central to the success of organizations in the contemporary economic environment, and this is reflected in the frequency with which the concerns of these fields are represented in business and management journals and in practitioner publications. Yet it is important to note that, although we can find the roots of both organizational learning and knowledge management in the 1960s, these fields have attracted significant attention only since the 1980s in management practice and only since the 1990s in academia. In part, this is the result of the changing nature of systems of production in the advanced nations – specifically, of the increased reliance on intellectual and knowledge-based assets as a source of competitiveness at the level of the firm and of the nation.

Interest in the social aspects of managing knowledge has resulted in a growing convergence between knowledge management and organizational learning; this convergence is nowhere more apparent than in the notion of communities of practice, which emerged from studies of situated learning (Lave and Wenger, 1991). Management practitioners and consultants have taken up the idea of communities of practice as a knowledge management technique. Simultaneously, the communities of practice framework has been adopted by scholars in various academic disciplines who are seeking to understand practice-based inter- and intra-organizational knowledge transfer and learning.

Indeed organizational learning and knowledge management are often considered together, as a number of handbooks and readers in the area demonstrate (see Prusak and Matson, 2006; Easterby-Smith and Lyles, 2011). Undoubtedly recent years have witnessed significant interaction between scholars of organizational learning and scholars of knowledge management, as illustrated by the concerns of the annual international

Organizational Learning, Knowledge and Capabilities Conference or by the content of multi-contributor volumes and journals in various fields – *Management Learning*, the *Journal of Knowledge Management*, and *The Learning Organization* among others. Nevertheless, these discussions are not confined to specialist journals; in fact the most influential contributions are published in mainstream management and organization journals such as the *Academy of Management Review*, *Human Relations*, *Journal of Management Studies*, *Organization Science*, *Organization Studies*, and *Strategic Management Journal*. The prominence of the topics of knowledge and learning in organizations in world-leading business and management journals underlines the centrality of these issues to management academics and practitioners. Moreover, as I will argue in later chapters, understanding knowledge management is also of importance to individuals and groups within and between organizations.

While recognizing the substantial interaction and areas of overlap between these related fields, Vera and Crossan provide a useful demarcation of the boundaries between organizational learning (OL) and organizational knowledge (OK) and between the learning organization (LO) and knowledge management (KM):

> OL focuses on learning as a process of change, while OK stresses knowledge as a resource that provides competitive advantage and studies the processes associated with its management. LO and KM share prescriptive views of how firms should effectively learn and manage knowledge. (2005: 127)

Despite recent convergence between these fields, differences remain. For example, as Easterby-Smith, Crossan, and Nicolini (2000) note, knowledge management is still led by technologists and employs the language of economics, whereas scholars with a human-resource orientation dominate organizational learning. This distinction explains the prevalence of knowledge management modules offered by information technology departments of universities. It is also apparent in library cataloguing systems. Look for books that privilege knowledge management in their title and you will find them located among those on information management and information systems, while those whose titles begin with organizational learning are to be found alongside texts on workers' skills and training.

As academic fields, both organizational learning and knowledge management emerged from rational thinking about information and knowledge, namely from the economics of organization and information systems management, before they moved to broader conceptualizations that take into account social dimensions and facilitate the development of less mechanical interpretations. Although their roots are similar, organizational learning and knowledge management have developed along different trajectories. Yet recent developments that view the firm as a cognitive system suggest a reconciliation of the two fields (Nooteboom, 2009). Table 2.2 provides a classification of these various fields in order to situate knowledge management among the related academic and practitioner fields. However, it is important to recognize the interaction and the blurring between the four areas. This book is concerned with knowledge management as both a practice and a field of study. Therefore the focus will be on the shaded area of Table 2.2. Even so, such are the connections between the four areas that frequently it will be necessary to touch upon issues concerning learning.

Table 2.2   Situating knowledge management

	Knowledge	Learning
Academic/theorizing	Organizational knowledge	Organizational learning
Practitioner/practice	Knowledge management	Learning organization

The place of knowledge management

This chapter has sought to situate knowledge management among its complementary and competing fields of practitioner and academic interest. Putting knowledge management in its place provides a foundation for what follows and offers a rationale for what might otherwise appear to be omissions in this short book. The development of the field of knowledge management has been (and continues to be) influenced by developments in the information technology domain. Yet, as noted in Chapter 1, key drivers of the adoption of knowledge management practices are to be found in popular policy debates about the knowledge economy – as well as in developments in the theory of the firm, which have drawn more and more attention to the role of knowledge as a core source of competitiveness.

Although knowledge management has become embedded in management practices, it has a reputation for incoherence and poor performance. This view is supported by the management consultancy Bain & Company's *Annual Survey of Management Tools*, which shows that knowledge management consistently falls short in its delivery of results for the companies surveyed (Rigby and Bilodeau, 2009). Nevertheless, an Economic Intelligence Unit survey of executives from around the world found that, of the 1,656 respondents, 43 per cent rated knowledge management as offering the greatest potential for productivity gains over the next 15 years (Economist Intelligence Unit, 2006: 4). Furthermore, knowledge management was ranked as the most important potential source of increased productivity.

Despite the importance of knowledge management in practice, the academic field has remained somewhat chaotic and in need of a clear direction (Lambe, 2011). This lack of academic coherence is also evident in the failure of knowledge management to establish itself as a consistent element of the business and management curriculum. While knowledge management modules and programmes are offered by many business schools, there is considerable inconsistency in the treatment of the area; some schools offer knowledge management degree programmes, while others merely offer consideration of the area as a component of broader modules on generalist business and management degree programmes. This failure to establish a firm position on the business and management curriculum is perhaps a reflection of the field's relative youth. Furthermore, knowledge management programmes and modules are often delivered in departments of computer science, information technology, and library management.

In light of the underperformance of knowledge management practices, there is an urgent need to raise the standing of knowledge management within business schools, in both teaching and research. Surely a key task for business schools should be to provide future management practitioners with the knowledge and skills required to realize the productivity gains available through efficient knowledge management.

Although there is a fair amount of consensus around what knowledge management is, how best to engage effectively in the process of knowledge management is more open to debate. The situation calls for greater clarification and for a better delineation of the field. This is not to argue for a narrowing of the field of study, but rather for a full recognition of the roots of knowledge management in a diverse range of social sciences: philosophy, economics, sociology, education, psychology, information and communications theory, and library and information studies (Wallace, 2007). Acknowledging this rich and interdisciplinary heritage provides access to the resources required to develop a comprehensive understanding of knowledge management in organization and in society. Moreover, the implications of knowledge management must be assessed from both an economic and a political perspective. It is this broad understanding of knowledge management that the present book seeks to impart; and I begin in the next chapter with an exploration of the extent to which knowledge can be managed.

Notes

1. For a highly accessible account of the development of information theory, see Gleick (2011).
2. See the project *The Domesday Book Online*, at http://www.domes daybook.co.uk/index.html (accessed 11 July 2014).

3

Knowledge Management?

A manager is responsible for the application and performance of knowledge.

Peter F. Drucker

The practice of knowledge management is predicated on the assumption that knowledge can be purposefully managed. The aim of this chapter is to explore the extent to which this assumption is valid. To achieve this it is necessary to look more closely at the nature of knowledge, the extent to which it can be managed, and the mechanisms that may be employed in any effective knowledge management process. Important aspects of knowledge that will be examined in this chapter are the difference between explicit or codified knowledge and tacit or implicit knowledge and the interactions and interdependencies between these two forms. In examining these differences, it is necessary to recognize two perspectives on knowledge. The first is the objectivist perspective, which treats knowledge as an object that can be owned and controlled like other assets. The second is the practice-based perspective, which considers knowledge to be socially constructed and embedded in practice. The difference between these two perspectives is captured well in the difference between 'knowledge' and 'knowing'. While from an objectivist stance knowledge may be captured in a book, from a practice perspective knowing is an ongoing social phenomenon. Nevertheless, it is vital to recognize that, in the complex organizations of the contemporary world, there are significant interdependencies between knowledge as an asset and knowing as a practice.

Developing a rigorous understanding of the nature of knowledge will provide a firm basis upon which to assess the extent to which it can be purposefully managed. Before progressing, it is necessary to consider the meaning of management in relation to knowledge.

Management and knowledge

The word 'manage' derives from the sixteenth-century Italian word *maneggiare* – to handle, control, or train horses, a compound ultimately based on the Latin word *manus* (hand). Today 'manage' refers to the act of exercising control over something, and, in relation to organizations, to controlling or coordinating resources in order to achieve specific outcomes. For our purposes, it is sufficient to define 'managing' as the process of organizing, controlling, or coordinating something, while management can be defined as a system of managing activities, the act of managing something, or those in charge of managing an organization.[1]

The process of managing can be undertaken at the individual, group, or organization level. At an individual level, we talk, for instance, about managing our time or managing our money. Management can also extend to the national or international level. In the aftermath of the global financial crisis of 2008, we frequently hear news reports about the poor economic management of specific financial ministers, particularly in countries like Greece and Portugal, while the finance ministers of the G20 countries are collectively urged to manage the global economy and help it out of its ongoing difficulties. Clearly, managing and the management systems that develop to facilitate the process of managing can range from simple to highly complex. Indeed, as Alvesson and Karreman (2001) note, it is possible to draw a distinction between the two modes of intervention necessary to manage an organization, namely coordination and control. The coordination mode requires minimal activity to facilitate collective action, whereas the control mode is broader in scope and requires structures that allocate activity, monitor, and evaluate individual and collective action.

Hence knowledge management is the process of organizing, controlling, and coordinating knowledge within organizations in order to achieve certain objectives. A number of definitions from academic and practitioner sources, presented in Table 3.1, confirm and elaborate on this understanding of knowledge management.

Unlike the academic definitions, which focus on knowledge, both practitioner definitions refer to information as something to be managed or generated. The Bain & Company definition is the more detailed one, particularly in terms of providing directions on how to manage knowledge. However, it also refers to the 'generation of useful, actionable and meaningful information'. Furthermore, this definition refers to intellectual assets in the form of 'intellectual base' and 'intellectual capital'. Thomas A. Stewart (1997: xx) defines intellectual capital succinctly as 'intellectual material – knowledge, information, intellectual property, experience – that can be put to use to create wealth'. Intellectual capital therefore resides in both tangible and intangible structures and systems within organizations. Important elements of an organization's intellectual and knowledge base exist in the individual and group experiences of its members. Yet Bain & Company prescribe the following actions for managers seeking to manage knowledge (Rigby, 2011: 32):

Table 3.1   Definitions of knowledge management from academic and practitioner sources

Author/s	Definitions of knowledge management
Academic sources	
van der Spek and Spijkervet (1997: 43)	'The explicit control and management of knowledge within an organization aimed at achieving the company's objectives.'
O'Leary (1998: 34)	'The formal management of knowledge for facilitating creation, access, and reuse of knowledge, typically using advanced technology.'
Bassi (1999: 424)	'The process of creating, capturing and using knowledge to enhance organizational performance.'
Liebowitz and Wilcox (1997: 1)	'The ability of organization to manage, store, value, and distribute knowledge.'
Scarbrough, Swan, and Preston (1999: 1)	'Any process or practice of creating, acquiring, capturing, sharing and using knowledge, wherever it resides, to enhance learning and performance in organizations.'
Hislop (2009: 59)	'An umbrella term which refers to any deliberate efforts to manage the knowledge of an organization's workforce, which can be achieved via a wide range of methods including directly, through the use of particular types of ICT, or more indirectly through the management of social processes, the structuring of organizations in particular ways or via the use of particular culture and people management practices.'
Practitioner sources	
American Productivity and Quality Centre (2014: 7)	'The application of a structured process to help information and knowledge flow to the right people at the right time so they can act more efficiently and effectively to find, understand, share, and use knowledge to create value.'
Bain & Company (Rigby, 2011: 32)	'Knowledge Management develops systems and processes to acquire and share intellectual assets. It increases the generation of useful, actionable and meaningful information and seeks to increase both individual and team learning. In addition, it can maximize the value of an organization's

Author/s	Definitions of knowledge management
Academic sources	
	intellectual base across diverse functions and disparate locations. Knowledge Management maintains that successful businesses are a collection not of products but of distinctive knowledge bases. This intellectual capital is the key that will give the company a competitive advantage with its targeted customers. Knowledge Management seeks to accumulate intellectual capital that will create unique core competencies and lead to superior results.'

- catalog and evaluate the organization's current knowledge base;
- determine which competencies will be key to future success and what base of knowledge is needed to build a sustainable leadership position therein;
- invest in systems and processes to accelerate the accumulation of knowledge;
- assess the impact of such systems on leadership, culture and hiring practices;
- codify new knowledge and turn it into tools and information that will improve both product innovation and overall profitability.

In contrast, Hislop's (2009: 59) definition of knowledge management focuses on efforts to manage the knowledge of an organization's workforce. It is the knowledge embedded in the workforce that can present the greatest challenge, because it requires the adoption of management approaches focused on coordinating highly skilled workers.

A knowledge-based view of the firm underlines the centrality of knowledge as a source of competitiveness and therefore provides a strong impetus for managers to develop methods, systems, and techniques to manage knowledge. However, can all knowledge within an organization be managed? While managers may be able to control knowledge that resides in databases, how can they control knowledge embedded in employees? Is it necessary to extract knowledge from employees through a process of codification in order to exert management control over it? If so, it is questionable whether current knowledge management practices are any different from the scientific management methods of the early twentieth century, which were inspired by the time and motion studies of Frederick Winslow Taylor (1856–1917). Such methods, together with the development of Fordist assembly line production methods, served to deskill workers (Braverman, 1974) in order to facilitate economically efficient mass production.

An alternative approach would be for management to focus on coordinating and facilitating knowledge workers rather than seeking direct control over knowledge. However, the appropriate management approach depends on the nature of the knowledge to be managed. Therefore it is necessary to look more closely at the nature of knowledge in organizations.

The nature of knowledge in organizations

Epistemology is a branch of philosophy concerned with our understanding of knowledge. Exploring the philosophy of knowledge is clearly beyond the scope of this book; nevertheless, it is worth noting that, in the western philosophical tradition, knowledge is defined as justified true belief. Yet, as noted in Chapter 1, truth depends on a given perspective or system of belief. For this reason, it is necessary to recognize that knowledge, understood as true and justified, is socially constructed. The reflections on the nature of knowledge that follow are only relevant to understanding knowledge management; hence they are predominantly concerned with, and limited to, knowledge in organizations.

In business and management literature knowledge has been variously defined. For instance, Davenport and Prusak define knowledge as

> a flux mix of framed experiences, values, contextual information and expert insight that provides a framework for evaluating and incorporating new experiences and information. It originates and is applied in the minds of knowers. In organizations, it often becomes embedded in routines, processes, practices, and norms. (1998: 5)

Similarly, Blackler argues that

> knowledge is multi-faceted and complex, being both situated and abstract, implicit and explicit, distributed and individual, physical and mental, developing and static, verbal and encoded. (1995: 1032)

Such descriptions encompass the many dimensions that characterize knowledge. However, a full appreciation of knowledge in an organizational context requires consideration of the various forms it may take and an examination of its diverse characteristics.

In discussions of the knowledge economy (see, for instance, OECD, 1996) a distinction is often made between the following types of knowledge:

- know-what;
- know-why;
- know-how;
- know-who.

Know-what is knowledge about 'facts' – such as the speed of light (299,792,458 metres per second) or the location of Mount Everest (coordinates: 27°59'17"N 86°55'31"E). Know-why is scientific knowledge of the principles and laws of nature; an example would be the relationship between mass and energy captured in Albert Einstein's formula $E = mc^2$. Knowledge in the form of know-what and know-why is close to information in that it can be codified, recorded, and embodied in an object. Know-what and know-why can be obtained by reading books and journals, by accessing databases, by watching DVDs, by attending lectures, and by using other opportunities to absorb the latest understandings of a particular topic. People absorb knowledge of this sort through individual cognitive processes such as attention, memory, information processing, and problem solving. Importantly, the cognitive capacity of individuals is influenced by the social context in which they develop and live. For instance, language, which is an essential tool required for understanding and processing information and knowledge, emerges in a social setting.

Know-how refers to skills or the ability to do something. Such knowledge is acquired over time, through a process of learning by doing (Arrow, 1962). Of course, the length of time required to learn a skill does depend on the complexity of the task. It is commonly accepted that practice is necessary to acquire a high level of competency. According to the sociologist Richard Sennett (2008), 10,000 hours of practice are required to develop a competence such as exercising a craft skill or playing a musical instrument. However, in addition to learning over time, the development of excellence in certain skills requires a particular aptitude. For example, I could play tennis every day but never become as skilful as Serena Williams, Roger Federer, or other top players. Many people study piano daily, but few attain the mastery of Lang Lang or concert pianists of his calibre. Nevertheless, through practice, skills become embedded in the minds and bodies of practitioners to such an extent that they may be unable to articulate fully how they perform certain tasks.

Because know-how is acquired and developed through practice, in order to attain a high level of competency, individuals must specialize. And, where specialist know-how is important, know-who will be essential – because, for specialization to be successful, it is necessary to bring individual specialists together with others in related fields. So, for example, to create and bring a new product to market requires a range of specialist skills from the areas of research and development (R&D), production, marketing, and sales and distribution. Having access to specialists in one or several of these areas is not sufficient. Specialists can be drawn together from a number of organizations. Increasingly organizations of all sorts are embedded in networks of relations with suppliers and customers or clients. Hence, success requires knowing-who knowledge – that is, knowing who knows what, and not just within the boundaries of the organization but also in the wider local and global commercial environment. For this reason, knowledge about who knows how to do specialist tasks is vital.

Although knowledge of the whereabouts of specialists can be recorded in a codified form such as in an address book or a database, know-who is much more than a list of contact details. An individual's name, email address, and telephone number do not ensure access to that person or to their knowledge. Indeed, with the help of the Internet, it is relatively easy to find the contact details of top people in most fields of knowledge, but securing access to their attention and time is more difficult. Having a recommendation from someone whom they know and trust can make the difference between a successful and a failed request for assistance. Of course, to identify and enlist the support of someone whom the specialist knows and trusts requires a social network of one's own. Consequently, know-who involves the formation of social relationships and the development of social capital, which provides access to experts and their knowledge. Like know-how, know-who develops over time, through experience and engagement in social practice. The growing importance of this type of knowledge is reflected in the rising academic interest in social capital, which the political scientist Robert Putnam (2000: 19), in a landmark study of the rise and fall of community in the USA, defines as 'connections among individuals – social networks and the norms of reciprocity and trustworthiness that arise from them'.

Trust becomes increasingly important in a knowledge-based economy. This is because it is difficult to judge the quality of a person's knowledge before engaging that person in a task. Hence it is necessary to trust experts in the sense of having confidence that they have the necessary skills to undertake the required task. Sometimes this trust arises from interpersonal relations: for instance, you may know the expert yourself, or you may know someone who has employed that expert in the past. In such cases you trust the expert because they have a good reputation. Willingness to trust an expert also derives from that person's possession of formal qualifications and membership of professional or trade bodies that monitor standards of knowledge. That is, our trust derives from the formal institutions to which the expert belongs. For instance, in the United Kingdom, the knowledge of a medical doctor is trusted because the position requires successful completion of a rigorous programme of education and training and because doctors are bound by the standards of their professional body, the British Medical Association, and by the regulation of the General Medical Council.

The distinction between know-what and know-why on the one hand, and know-how and know-who on the other rests largely on the degree to which knowledge can be made explicit or codified. Knowledge is codified if it is recorded or transmitted in the form of symbols or sounds (for example, through writing, drawings, or the spoken word) or embodied in a tangible form (for example, in machinery or tools). By capturing knowledge in an explicit form, codification separates it from the knower; thus, when knowledge is externalized in this way, it becomes a commodity or an asset, just like other materials used in the production process. Knowledge becomes an object, and in this process it acquires the potential to be seen as objective – in the sense that it can become factual and exists independently of any individual. This kind of knowledge contrasts with the knowledge attached to an individual or group of individuals, which can be interpreted as opinion and viewed as subjective.

Nevertheless, for knowledge to be classified as objective, it must be independently verifiable. But even facts can be open to question, as their interpretation depends on the frames of reference employed in their presentation as well as in their reception. This state of affairs is captured well in an episode of the 2009 US television sitcom *Better Off Ted*, which is set in the R&D division of a giant malevolent corporation. Linda is a 'product tester' and, in response to her lack of confidence in a new scented light bulb when she discovers that it smells of rotting meat after prolonged use, her department head and mentor, Veronica, declares: 'Those are just facts and facts are just opinions and opinions can be wrong. The only thing that is never wrong is confidence.' Clearly, even so-called objective knowledge is open to interpretation, and its meaning can be influenced by the way it is presented. This is often apparent in political rivals' use of the same statistics to support opposing arguments.

The tacit dimension and its connection to explicit knowledge

When knowledge is not codified, it is described as 'implicit' or 'tacit' knowledge. Such knowledge is acquired via the informal take-up of learning behaviour and procedures. In their study of organizational knowledge, Nonaka and Takeuchi (1995) identify two dimensions of tacit knowledge. First, there is the technical dimension encompassing skills or crafts. Second, there is the cognitive dimension consisting of schemata, mental models, and beliefs that shape the way individuals perceive the world around them. Tacit knowledge is, then, very much embedded in individuals and groups.

Tacit knowledge is personal in the sense that we all see the world in different ways. Our understanding of our surroundings is developed through our experience over the course of our lives. Particular beliefs and understandings are inculcated in us from our earliest days. These come, for example, from our relationships with family members, friends, and teachers; or they may emanate from religious and political organizations. Indeed everything that we come into contact with leaves an impression on us, however slight or significant. It is through a lens shaped by these experiences that we encounter and 'see' new artefacts, people, theories, ideologies, and so on. Two people with very similar experiences will share a high degree of similarity in their interpretations of the world, while individuals with very different experiences may have highly divergent understandings of the same phenomenon. We all see the world differently, but some people see it more differently than others. Clearly one's cultural and historical background will influence one's understandings – as will one's level of formal education and one's prior experience.

Through the process of codification, knowledge is made explicit and reduced to information that can be transformed into knowledge by all those who have access to the appropriate code or framework of analysis. Hence explicit and codified knowledge can be shared and transferred across time and space. However, in order to share such knowledge, an individual has to make an initial irreversible investment to acquire the relevant code. Importantly, such a retrieval structure may be made up of both explicit and tacit knowledge. Language, for example, is a form of codification and a retrieval structure – but, of course, knowledge of language is both codified, in terms of vocabulary and rules of grammar, and tacit, since the meaning attached to words changes with the context of their use – and inflections added in the act of speaking can significantly influence meaning too. All those who have learnt a language in the classroom will confront these tacit aspects when they come to put their linguistic knowledge into practice in the real world – a world that, unlike textbooks, is dynamic and constantly evolving and where meaning can vary depending on context, location, and the level of familiarity between interlocutors.

It is wrong to think that all tacit knowledge can be codified and thereby made explicit. In his book on *The Tacit Dimension*, Michael Polanyi (1967: 4) offers the valuable insight that 'we know more than we can tell', in the sense that tacit knowing consists of knowledge that is indeterminate and its content cannot be explicitly stated. Polanyi demonstrates this point in relation to the possession of a skill:

> If I know how to ride a bicycle or how to swim, this does not mean that I can tell how I manage to keep my balance on a bicycle, or keep afloat when swimming. I may not have the slightest idea of how I do this, or even an entirely wrong or grossly imperfect idea of it, and yet go on cycling or swimming merrily. Nor can it be said that I know how to bicycle or swim and yet do *not* know how to coordinate the complex pattern of muscular acts by which I do my cycling or swimming. I both know how to carry out these performances as a whole and also know how to carry out the elementary acts which constitute them, though I cannot tell what these acts are. This is due to the fact that I am only subsidiarily aware of these things and our subsidiary awareness of a thing *may not suffice to make it identifiable*. (1966: 4)

Consequently, an important characteristic of tacit knowledge is that it cannot be articulated and is therefore uncodifiable. A distinction can be made between articulable knowledge that is codified and articulable knowledge that remains uncodified (Cowan, David, and Foray, 2000). Uncodified articulable knowledge is often assumed to be tacit; but it is different from tacit knowledge in that it is codifiable. The codification of articulable knowledge depends on the economic incentives to codify. In situations where knowledge is changing rapidly, it does not make sense to invest resources in the codification of knowledge, because that knowledge will soon be obsolete. In other cases resisting codification may be a strategy to protect knowledge, because, once codified, it can be more easily circulated – both within an organization and to competitors.

The distinction between tacit and explicit or codified knowledge is a significant one, as is the relationship between the two types of knowledge. There is sometimes a tendency to see knowledge as either explicit or tacit; however, this is much too simplistic. Knowledge is rarely completely tacit or completely codified. For, as Polanyi argues, 'while tacit knowledge can be possessed by itself, explicit knowledge must rely on being tacitly understood and applied. Hence all knowledge is *either tacit* or *rooted in tacit knowledge*. A *wholly* explicit knowledge is unthinkable' (1966: 7).

The relationship between tacit and explicit knowledge is complex and contributes to the dynamic nature of knowledge. Nonaka and Takeuchi (1995: 61), elaborating on their idea of knowledge conversion in the context of the organization, stress the complementary nature of tacit and explicit knowledge, arguing that these two types 'interact with and interchange into each other in the creative activities of human beings'. Moreover, these authors' dynamic model of knowledge creation assumes that, through social interaction, knowledge circulates between tacit and explicit forms and new knowledge is developed in this conversion process. Importantly, knowledge conversion 'is a "social" process *between* individuals and not confined *within* an individual' (1995: 61). Consequently knowledge transfer through socialization contributes to the creation of new knowledge.

Explicit knowledge, with the appropriate contractual arrangements, may be transferred between individuals or organizations in a codified tangible embodiment such as blueprints or patents, in machinery, as part of licensing and franchise agreements, or through trade between agents. Tacit knowledge, though, often requires considerable time to acquire. For instance, it may be gained during an apprenticeship or a period of learning by doing. Even when knowledge is explicit and available in a codified form, much of the tacit element remains uncodified, and consequently the transfer of the codified knowledge alone may fail to facilitate the successful transfer of knowledge. The economic historian David Landes (1999) provides the following excellent illustration of the difficulties of knowledge transferred through codified knowledge. During the First World War, the French, needing an additional supply of their 75-mm field guns, sent their blueprints to the USA. However, the Americans could only produce guns of the required quality after a team of French workers went to show them how to make them. Even when sophisticated computer-aided methods of recording codified knowledge are available, tacit knowledge remains vital in the production of military equipment, as MacKenzie and Spinardi's (1995) study of the diffusion of nuclear weapons demonstrates. There are, then, elements of tacit knowledge, or know-how, that can only be transferred successfully through a process of demonstration, or show-how, facilitated through face-to-face contact between the transmitter and the receiver (Roberts, 2000).

The distinction between explicit or codified and tacit or implicit knowledge is paralleled by that between knowledge as something that is fixed in the form of an asset or object and knowledge that is embedded in a process or practice – knowing rather than knowledge. This key distinction has been portrayed by academics through explorations of knowledge in various contrasting forms. Table 3.2 summarizes the common characteristics associated with explicit and tacit knowledge in the academic literature.

Table 3.2 Contrasting characteristics of explicit and tacit knowledge

Explicit knowledge	Tacit knowledge
Codified	Implicit/non-codified/non-codifiable
Knowledge	Knowing
An object	A practice or a process
Know-what and know-why	Know-how and know-who
Canonical	Non-canonical
Propositional	Prescriptive
Universal	Context-specific

Tacit knowledge is often associated with individuals and seen as personal. In contrast, explicit knowledge is viewed as impersonal and therefore more easily distributed between individuals. Yet tacit knowledge need not be merely personal, nor explicit knowledge solely collective. J.-C. Spender (1996) presents a useful typology of organizational knowledge in which he makes a distinction between explicit and tacit knowledge at both the individual and the social level. According to his analysis, explicit knowledge can exist at the individual level in a conscious form, or at the social or collective level in an objective form. Hence objectified knowledge, embodied perhaps in a book or manual that is available to a collection of individuals, may also reside within an individual in a conscious manner. For example, through studying an organization's customer care manual, which sets out the procedures on how to deal with customers, a sales person knows consciously the steps to follow in order to deal appropriately with a customer complaint. Spender argues that tacit knowledge at an individual level is automatic; it is unconsciously held and employed in everyday activity, while at the social level tacit knowledge is collectively held: such forms of knowledge develop through the collective use of language and action.

By drawing a distinction between the individual and the social level, Spender's typology provides a deeper understanding of explicit and tacit knowledge within organizations. However, in a recent book entitled *Tacit and Explicit Knowledge*, Harry Collins (2010), an internationally renowned scholar in the field of the sociology of scientific knowledge and an expert on tacit knowledge, takes the analysis one step further. Collins begins from a focus on explicit knowledge and puts Polanyi's idea of all knowledge being tacit or rooted in tacit knowledge into the wider historical context of the existence of knowledge:

> Though the tension between tacit and explicit goes back at least as far as the Greeks, it was modernism in general and the computer revolution in particular that made the explicit seem easy and the tacit seem obscure. But nearly the entire history of the universe, and that includes the parts played by animals and the first humans, consists of things going along quite nicely without anyone *telling* anything to anything or anyone. There is, then, nothing strange about things being done but not being told – it is normal life. What is strange is that anything *can* be told. (Collins, 2010: 7)

Collins goes on to argue that the idea that tacit knowledge was special could not occur to anyone until about the middle of the twentieth century, when explicability became commonplace. In the contemporary world, the explicit rather than the tacit is taken to be the norm. Indeed the world is driven by the explicit knowledge required to manage the huge corporations and government administrations that are a feature of the twenty-first century. Collins identifies four ways in which knowledge can be made explicable: first, by elaboration; second, by transformation; third, as mechanization; and finally, as explanation. Nevertheless, some knowledge remains tacit.

Collins elaborates three types of tacit knowledge. The first is 'weak' or relational. This is tacit knowledge that could be made explicit but is not, for reasons that are not related to the nature and location of knowledge or the way humans are made. For example, sometimes knowledge that could be told is deliberately kept hidden. An example would be a business that keeps knowledge of production methods secret for commercial reasons. In addition, relational tacit knowledge includes ostensive knowledge, which can be learnt only with reference to some object or practice, because its description in language would be too complex to be articulated and comprehended by humans. Collins also refers to logistically demanding knowledge and to knowledge that is kept hidden unintentionally or is actually unrecognized. He argues that, because the reason why it is not explicit is contingent on things that can be changed, relational tacit knowledge can be made explicit, although not all at once.

The second form of tacit knowledge identified by Collins is somatic. It is tacit because of the way it is inscribed in the material of the body and of the brain. Collins uses Polanyi's bicycle-riding example, quoted above, to illustrate the nature of somatic tacit knowledge and argues that what stops bicycle riding from being carried out according to explicit instructions is the limit on the speed of our brains and of our reactions. Hence we have to acquire the knowledge to ride a bicycle through learning by doing. In principle somatic tacit knowledge can be made explicit, yet it remains technically beyond our capacity to express it in rules that could be executed by humans. Nevertheless, somatic knowledge is expressible in rules that can be executed by machines. So, for example, in the case of the balancing required to ride a bicycle, this skill can already be captured in programs for machines, which actually perform balancing tasks better than humans do.

For Collins, what remains beyond the reach of the expressible is the social dimension. This gives rise to the third type of tacit knowledge, which he describes as 'strong' or collective. It is the type of knowledge that individuals acquire by being embedded in society. Strong collective tacit knowledge is the property of society rather than of the individual. Collins argues that the ability to draw upon strong tacit knowledge, that is, to be a parasite on the body of the social, is a uniquely human characteristic.

Through the notion of 'social Cartesianism', Collins seeks to capture the uniqueness of humans with respect to their ability to draw on strong tacit knowledge and to employ their own resources so as to act in concert with what other humans are doing. Social Cartesianism is quite different from the doctrine of Cartesianism elaborated by the seventeenth-century French philosopher René Descartes, who viewed the mind as being wholly separate from the corporeal body. Rather social Cartesianism refers to the abilities of humans to draw on societal resources that arise from our mutual participation in society as a larger organism. Crucially humans, unlike machines, understand the social context and can therefore engage in polymorphic actions – that is, actions that are responsive to context and meaning. The need for actions to function effectively in social environments ensures the persistence of strong, collective tacit knowledge. For Collins, this type remains the irreducible element of tacit knowledge and therefore is uncodifiable, while the other types are, at least in principle, merely uncodified.

The nature of knowledge at an individual, an organizational, and a societal level has implications for the extent to which knowledge may be actively managed – and for whether its management can take place through coordination or control. We now turn to the question of managing knowledge in organizations.

Approaches to managing knowledge in organizations

Early efforts to manage knowledge in organizations tended to treat it as an asset or object that could be moved around the organization like any other tangible resource. Where knowledge was intangible, the management imperative was to capture it in a tangible form in order to exert control over it. The process of capturing knowledge through the codification strategy employed by some companies in the 1990s is well described by Hansen, Nohria, and Tierney (1999) – in relation to large consultancy companies like Andersen Consulting and Ernst and Young – as a 'people to documents' approach. Ralph Poole, director of Ernst and Young's Centre for Business Knowledge, presents this approach as follows:

> After removing the client-sensitive information, we develop 'knowledge objects' by pulling key pieces of knowledge such as interview guides, work schedules, benchmark data, and market segmentation analyses out of the documents and storing them in the electronic repository for people to use. (Quoted in Hansen et al., 1999: 108)

Such strategies depended upon the availability of sophisticated computer databases and expert systems, which facilitate the codification of complex knowledge-based activities. When successfully implemented, they allowed the organization's members to search for and retrieve knowledge without the need to identify and communicate with the individual who had originally developed the relevant 'knowledge object'. In this way consultancy organizations could benefit from economies of scale in the use of knowledge and could thereby reduce their costs and improve their profitability. Central to the popularity of such approaches was the falling cost of computing and electronic storage capacity, as well as the increasing scope for networking, which came to the fore in the 1990s and facilitated global access to such resources. Moreover, the scope offered by computers for the collection, collation, and analysis of data encouraged this trend. Certainly computers offer great opportunities; but, in order to be able to apply the power of computers to knowledge, the latter must be reducible to information in a cost-effective manner, in other words it must be codifiable.

Yet it is important to note that, even in the late 1990s, some companies took an alternative approach to knowledge management. For example, as Hansen and colleagues (1999) detail in what they refer to as the 'personalization strategy' adopted by strategy consultants like Bain & Company, Boston Consulting Group, and McKinsey, the focus was on the dialogue between individuals rather than on the codification of knowledge. Instead of developing knowledge objects, the personalization strategy facilitated the transfer of knowledge through brainstorming and in one-to-one sessions. According to these authors' analysis, whether a consulting company adopts a codification or a personalization knowledge management strategy depends on whether it is providing a standardized service – where knowledge objects like interview guides and work schedules can be reused – or a personalized service – which requires developing new knowledge for each client.

Within organizations, knowledge may be embedded in tangible assets like machinery, operations manuals, databases, finished goods, or services as well as in people and intangible assets like brands, reputation, or organizational routines. Tangible assets can be seen, measured, and evaluated in ways that are not available for intangible assets. Take an input into the production process – a ton of oranges intended to produce cartons of fresh orange juice. Here it is possible for a manager to assess the quality of the oranges – whether they are ripe, fresh, sweet, and so on. These qualities can be evaluated through direct physical examination and, as the nature of oranges remains fairly constant, managers learn from experience to assess them with a high degree of accuracy. Compare this with the assessment of a knowledge input such as the skills of a marketing expert charged with promoting the sale of the organization's fresh orange juice. How does the manager assess the suitability of the expert? The manager does not have access to the knowledge possessed by the marketing expert – and this is why such an expert is employed. Moreover, the manager will not gain this knowledge over time, because the expertise is continually changing due to the ongoing development of media outlets and to the changing social context, which has the capacity to impact on trends in orange juice consumption. The manager must rely on the expert's credentials – perhaps accredited degrees and membership of the Chartered Institute of Marketing, past successes, or recommendations from previous employers.

When seeking to coordinate and control highly skilled knowledge workers like marketing experts, managers encounter a problem of asymmetric information: economists refer to this as an agency problem (Jensen and Meckling, 1976). The worker has greater knowledge about how to conduct some specific but important tasks for the organization than the person charged with their management. This presents significant challenges for the management of the knowledge embedded in employees. Traditional hierarchical forms and structures of management based on the exercise of authority are not the most appropriate means of coordinating the activities of highly skilled knowledge workers. It is for this reason that Paul Adler (2001) suggests community forms of organization as an alternative in knowledge-based organizations. While knowledge as an asset may be managed through traditional approaches, knowledge in the form of knowing in practice requires alternative approaches.

Given the increasing emphasis placed on the tacit dimension of knowledge since the beginning of the twenty-first century, practice-based approaches to understanding and managing knowledge have attracted increasing attention (Gherardi, 2006). Among these, the communities of practice approach, which derives from a theory of situated learning (Lave and Wenger, 1991), has become a popular method of knowledge management. Practice-based approaches recognize that organizational knowledge exists in a social context; organizational knowing is something that occurs in practice; and knowledge is transferred and created through interaction between people working together. Initial formulations of practice-based approaches recognized that knowledge practices could not be managed directly; rather they emerged spontaneously in a socially situated context. Even so, Brown and Duguid (1991) argue that an organization's internal environment can be managed so as to encourage the development of such communities.

However, there has been a gradual appropriation of community by management in some organizations. Indeed the application of the communities of practice approach to knowledge management has itself been implemented in a rather mechanistic and managerial fashion. This has been encouraged by the publication of a number of practical guides to knowledge management through communities (see, for example, Wenger, McDermott, and Snyder, 2002; Saint-Onge and Wallace, 2003), as well as by the proliferation of consultancy services aimed at cultivating knowledge communities. These developments run counter to the original idea of communities of practice as socially situated sites of learning. The mechanistic application of practice-based approaches tends to privilege management priorities, thereby undermining the benefits that can arise from allowing social interactions to determine the knowledge activities of the community. In this way the application of the whole approach risks diminishing the potential contribution of communities to the effective creation, acquisition, and exchange of knowledge. Hence adopting practice-based approaches to knowledge management requires a strategy focused on coordination and facilitation rather than on authority and control.

The turn towards practice-based approaches, which places weight on the tacit elements of knowledge, raises the danger of neglecting the management of explicit knowledge. The handling of an organization's intellectual property in the form of proprietary databases, patents, copyrights, and trademarks remains a significant knowledge management challenge for many companies. Given the huge volume of information that many organizations are required to collect, collate, analyse, and disseminate, the efficient management of such knowledge assets is highly important. It is therefore necessary for organizations to adopt the appropriate balance of knowledge management methods according to the significance of the various types of knowledge employed. Furthermore, the link between explicit and tacit knowledge in any organization should not be overlooked; there are significant interdependencies that must be recognized and managed.

To illustrate the relationship between explicit and tacit knowledge, we only have to think about our own knowledge management activity. Many of you who read this book will be knowledge workers, or at least a good portion of your work will involve the use of knowledge. If you are a university student, there is a good chance that you are preparing yourself for a career as a knowledge worker. Let me explore my own engagement in knowledge management as an illustration. Everything I do as a university professor involves knowledge of some sort. On a daily basis I engage in the collection, collation, analysis, and dissemination of knowledge. For example, to prepare lectures and journal articles, I draw on knowledge I gained through experience and formal education, as well as from a wide range of other sources, too numerous to list in full: academic articles, daily newspapers, Internet blogs and websites, textbooks, news and current affairs television and radio programmes, fiction and documentary films, conversations with family, friends, colleagues, students, and strangers – in short, everything that delivers information to me in my everyday life. My employer makes some of these resources available to me, while I access others through my own personal and professional sources. Consequently, in performing my job, I rely on my own and my employer's knowledge management structures, such as libraries, databases, and academic communities. Through these sources I find materials and ideas that provide inputs into my knowledge outputs – which include books, journal articles, or the delivery of lectures and research presentations. I am not only exposed to explicit knowledge, I also benefit from attending seminars, workshops, and conferences and interacting with the academic community in my own institution and beyond. Importantly, interaction with other academics – whether face-to-face at conferences, or through email discussions or Skype meetings – helps me to improve my own knowledge and to collaborate in the creation of new knowledge. Hence, in managing my own knowledge, I make use of tacit knowledge, for example of who knows what, and I depend upon explicit knowledge structures like the library maintained by my employer. Reflecting on the knowledge work that I do makes it clear that both explicit and tacit knowledge are vital to my work. While tacit knowledge may be an important aspect of my expertise, it is necessary to recognize that the realization of valuable outputs from this expertise also requires access to explicit and codified knowledge, whether this comes from my own private resources, my employer's, or the public domain.

Conclusion

A fundamental criticism of knowledge management derives from the view that knowledge cannot be managed. For instance, Alvesson and Karreman (2001: 995) argue 'that knowledge is an ambiguous, unspecific and dynamic phenomenon, intrinsically related to meaning, understanding and process, and therefore difficult to manage. There is thus a contradiction between knowledge and management.' They go on to suggest 'that knowledge management is as likely, if not more so, to operate as a practice of managing people or information than [*sic*] as a practice attuned towards facilitating knowledge creation'. Scholars and practitioners commonly conflate or confuse knowledge and information, so that efforts to manage knowledge focus on the management of information. Yet a major element in the management of knowledge, as Alvesson and Karreman suggest, is to do with managing people; for it is often in its employees that an organization's intellectual capital resides.

Although not manageable in the same way as tangible resources, knowledge workers can be supported through access to appropriate knowledge infrastructures. In my case, for instance, access to library resources and to academic colleagues is vital. Managers can facilitate the development of libraries and academic communities by providing the necessary resources. Clearly, managing the knowledge embedded in people and in the communities they participate in requires the management of people rather than the direct management of knowledge. Therefore knowledge management systems that support knowledge workers by providing them with timely access to appropriate explicit knowledge and with the conditions needed for acquiring tacit knowledge are essential.

Knowledge management includes a diverse range of activities – from the acquisition, retention, and transfer of knowledge in the form of tangible assets to the support, coordination, and management of knowledge workers. In the next chapter we will focus on the acquisition, retention, and transfer of knowledge; and we will explore how the nature of the knowledge influences the management of these processes.

Note

1. For a detailed discussion of the nature and rise of management, see Grey (2013).

4

Knowledge Acquisition, Retention, and Transfer

If you have knowledge, let others light their candles at it.

Margaret Fuller

It is clear from the previous chapters that knowledge is complex and its management is no easy task. However, before knowledge can be managed, it must be acquired. Once it has been acquired, its management necessitates methods to retain it within the organization as well as mechanisms for its transfer between internal members and relevant external parties – such as customers and suppliers. For knowledge to be a source of competitiveness for an organization, it must be applied. Hence knowledge must be transferred to and absorbed by relevant individuals and groups, so that they may apply it purposefully to sustain and improve the competitive performance of the organization. Knowledge, in and of itself, will not provide a competitive advantage; it is only when it is applied that this potential is released. The main purpose of this chapter is to explore the acquisition, retention, and transfer of knowledge from the perspective of managing knowledge for competitiveness. Negative consequences that could result, both for individuals and for society, from the drive for competitiveness through knowledge management practices will also be highlighted.

The ability of an organization and its members to acquire, retain, and transfer knowledge is influenced by the nature of the knowledge involved, as well as by the capacities of the organization's workforce and infrastructure, including its technological resources. The processes of knowledge acquisition, retention, and transfer will be examined from the standpoint of both explicit and tacit knowledge. A key point that we need to recognize is that these types of knowledge are interdependent; hence examining the transfer of explicit or tacit knowledge independently will not suffice. It is necessary to expose the symbiotic nature of these forms of knowledge. Moreover, an exploration of the transfer of knowledge requires a recognition that this process occurs at various levels; within an organization, this implies that it occurs between individuals, groups, and departments. Knowledge transfer within the organization is labelled 'intra-organizational knowledge transfer'. Furthermore, organizations engage with clients and suppliers as well as with competitors, sector-specific organizations and business, and regulatory institutions. In so doing, they transfer knowledge to external parties. This kind of knowledge transfer is labelled 'inter-organizational knowledge transfer'.

The chapter considers knowledge acquisition, retention, and transfer one by one. Clearly these are often interlinked, and these connections are highlighted here. In relation to the retention of knowledge, the chapter reviews issues concerning its protection – specifically, intellectual property rights (IPRs). The importance of trust and information and communications technologies (ICTs) as facilitators of knowledge transfer is also examined.

Knowledge acquisition

A key element related to the acquisition of knowledge is creativity and innovation (taken together as one), in the sense that knowledge is acquired through the development of new knowledge in the organization. This type of knowledge acquisition forms an important aspect of knowledge management, so much so that it will receive detailed consideration in Chapter 5. For the purposes of this chapter, the kind of knowledge acquisition to be explored is acquisition from the external environment. Organizations acquire knowledge through the employment of new workers who bring knowledge with them or through existing workers who absorb knowledge from the external environment. Organizations may also acquire knowledge through mergers and acquisitions, or else through the purchase of knowledge-intensive services like consultancy, research and development (R&D) outsourcing, and externally provided training programmes. In addition, knowledge may be acquired through the purchase of access to databases or machinery and equipment in which knowledge is embedded.

The various different channels through which an organization obtains knowledge can favour particular types of knowledge. For instance, the organization may purchase a database of information concerning potential clients, from which its members can extract information and combine it with their existing knowledge to produce new knowledge that supports the organization's competitiveness. This example illustrates the acquisition of explicit knowledge in a codified form, through a commercial exchange. Similarly, a consultancy company may provide a report on a particular aspect of the organization's market or management structures. Here again, knowledge is embedded in a codified form. Furthermore, its acquisition can be of benefit to the organization only if that knowledge is applied.

An example that illustrates these types of knowledge acquisition is the purchase of services from the customer science company Dunnhumby Ltd, employed by Tesco in the mid-1990s to build its databank of customer information through the Tesco Clubcard. To obtain a Clubcard, a customer must provide items of personal information such as address, telephone numbers, age, gender, size of household, household members' ages, and household dietary requirements. When the customer presents the Clubcard at the checkout, the information on the items purchased is collected along with the date, time, and location of the transaction. In return for engaging in the data collection process, customers are given rewards, for instance discounts off specific goods and vouchers that can be used on all purchases. Through the Clubcard initiative, Tesco has accumulated a vast set of information on customers and their purchasing habits that can be mined to develop knowledge from which it is possible to build better customer experiences and to foster loyalty. It is estimated that Dunnhumby Ltd has helped to save Tesco some £350 million a year (Brown, 2010). Indeed, such is the importance of Dunnhumby to Tesco's success that it is now wholly owned by the global supermarket giant.

According to its website, Dunnhumby analyses data from over 660 million customers worldwide, to gain valuable insights about their desires, locations, and price preferences.[1] In this way Dunnhumby is able to assist client companies in meeting the needs of their customers. Information is extracted from the data collected through mechanisms such as the Tesco Clubcard. It then becomes knowledge when it is considered in the context of existing knowledge about customers. Through the employment of companies like Dunnhumby Ltd, organizations acquire explicit knowledge through commercial exchange. Such exchanges involve the movement of knowledge in codified forms like reports, which may be accompanied by the movement of people – for example, to deliver the findings of a report or to consult with the client company.

When compared to the acquisition of explicit knowledge, the acquisition of tacit knowledge usually involves greater emphasis on the movement of people and their interaction within and outside of the organization. For instance, the employment of new staff may bring novel know-how to the organization; or existing workers may develop their own tacit knowledge through engagement in external personal and professional communities, and then they would use it in their employment. Accountants and marketers, for example, engage in the networks that exist around their professional associations, like the Chartered Institute of Management Accountants or the Chartered Institute of Marketing. By attending conferences, seminars, and workshops hosted by these professional associations, they acquire new knowledge, which can be brought to bear on the work that they perform in the organization.

Mergers and acquisitions can also be an important mechanism for gaining access to tacit bodies of knowledge, because they usually involve the acquisition of individual workers and groups. Of course, explicit knowledge is also acquired in this way; for example, the knowledge embodied in patents, databases, and machinery may be among the assets acquired. Nevertheless, tacit knowledge can be more difficult for an organization to acquire and transfer through its members. This is because tacit knowledge resides within individuals or groups and its acquisition, retention, and transfer are dependent on the social interaction between individuals, which is mediated by sociocultural norms and practices that are beyond the organization's direct control.

Acquiring knowledge is one thing; to benefit from its acquisition, an organization must possess the capacity to absorb and apply this new knowledge. Cohen and Levinthal refer to this feature as 'absorptive capacity', which they define as an ability 'to recognize the value of new external information, assimilate it, and apply it to commercial ends' (1990: 128). Building on this conceptualization and on earlier ones, Zahra and George go further, arguing that absorptive capacity is 'a set of organizational routines and processes by which firms acquire, assimilate, transform, and exploit knowledge to produce a dynamic organizational capability' (2002: 186). From their perspective, the ability to absorb knowledge can be divided into a *potential* absorptive capacity – the ability to acquire and assimilate knowledge – and a *realized* absorptive capacity – the ability to make use of the knowledge that has been absorbed. There is, then, an important distinction between acquiring and applying knowledge.

The motivation to absorb new knowledge is driven by the benefits that its application can provide. While an organization's absorptive capacity is based on prior related knowledge, ultimately it depends on its employees' absorptive capacity (Cohen and Levinthal, 1990). Individuals within organizations can thus have important roles in facilitating the realization of the benefits from the acquisition, assimilation, transformation, and exploitation of external knowledge. This is especially the case for individuals with roles that have gate-keeping or boundary-spanning functions. Hence, such individuals are in positions of power with regard to influencing what knowledge is acquired by the organization and what knowledge is neglected or ignored.

Alongside the individual's role in developing a firm's ability to acquire and absorb knowledge, it is also necessary to consider the organization's internal processes and its relationships with external parties. For instance, Lane and Lubatkin (1998) found that the ability to absorb knowledge between organizations depends on the similarity of knowledge bases, high informalities, centralization of research activities, similar compensation practices, and joint research communities. Moreover, they argue that the organization's ability to learn can be more significant than R&D investment in terms of the organization's competitiveness.

Many of the challenges evident in the acquisition of knowledge are also present for recipients in the knowledge transfer process. For this reason further consideration will be given later in this chapter to the acquisition of knowledge in the context of knowledge transfer. However, in the next section we turn to the challenges of retaining knowledge once it has been acquired.

Knowledge retention

According to the knowledge-based view of the firm (Grant, 1996), knowledge is the most important source of competitive advantage because it is both difficult to imitate and socially complex. Yet the knowledge capabilities of an organization only provide an important source of sustained competitiveness if access to them is restricted. If a particular knowledge base is widely available, there is no distinctive advantage to be gained through its acquisition. Therefore, to fully exploit the benefits of newly acquired knowledge that holds the potential to offer competitive advantage, an organization must restrict its use, thereby preventing its widespread dissemination. Alternatively, the organization could gain a proprietary right over the use of the knowledge in order to control its diffusion beyond the organization's boundaries. When referring to knowledge retention, then, it is important to consider how one stores and protects knowledge so as to prevent or control its widespread dissemination. Consequently this section considers the mechanisms employed to store and protect knowledge and how these mechanisms vary according to the explicit or tacit nature of knowledge.

Before going on, however, it is important to note that knowledge that is valuable today may hold little value tomorrow. Knowledge can quickly become outdated. For example, the introduction of new products such as the iPod in the recorded music sector, or of new business models like Amazon's online retailing platform, has significantly changed the dynamics of competition in the respective markets. As a result, the knowledge advantages held by competitors have been rapidly eroded. Consequently, while organizations can develop systems to retain and protect knowledge, radical innovations in the external environment can undermine their efforts. It is for this reason that organizations must, alongside these efforts to retain and protect knowledge, invest in the acquisition of new knowledge through creativity and innovation.

The idea of storing knowledge suggests that it can be accumulated for current and future use. Through codification, knowledge can be stored and therefore disseminated across time and space. The codification of knowledge is not just of significance to businesses but to society as a whole. Knowledge is stored and transferred from one generation to another through training and sophisticated systems of education as well as through the libraries, actual and virtual, upon which these systems depend. Knowledge is also stored and transferred through language and cultural norms and practices and routines. To be able to access the knowledge available in a library, it is necessary not only to understand the idea of a library and the books that it may hold, but also to be able to read in the language in which knowledge is codified in the pages of the books or on the visual displays. Without knowledge of the code – that is, the language – and without the ability to read the written language, codified knowledge is inaccessible. For instance, the capacity to access knowledge embedded in ancient Egyptian hieroglyphs was lost until the discovery of the Rosetta Stone in 1799, which contains the same inscription in both ancient Greek (a known language) and ancient Egyptian hieroglyphs. Through a process of translation and decoding that took scholars over 20 years, ancient Egyptian hieroglyphs became known once again, thus enabling access to the traces of knowledge left by this ancient civilization.

Libraries are systems of managing knowledge through the collection and storage of codified knowledge and data. In this capacity, libraries are information management systems. Until the widespread diffusion of the computer, information management was very much concerned with the collection of material, namely paper-based documents, files, and records. In fact information management systems range from the address book, which collects the names and contact details of loved ones, friends, work colleagues, and business associates, to the British Library, which holds copies of every book published in the United Kingdom and Ireland – and much more. The widespread distribution of computers in the 1980s gave rise to sophisticated information systems comprised of networks of information technology (IT) hardware and software, which are used to collect, filter, process, and distribute data. As computing power has increased exponentially, so too has the capacity of information systems. In today's world of multimedia-enabled smart mobile telephones, the Internet, cloud computing, and social media, information management systems have reached into every aspect of business and social life.

Access to knowledge on the scale now possible is of huge benefit, because such access has the potential to contribute to increased productivity and creativity in the workforce. Those seeking to solve problems are now able to draw on an enormous body of information and ideas. The combination of codification and computing power assists in the creation of new knowledge, making possible the analysis of data in ways that were previously unthinkable. For instance, the application of computing power to assist in the decoding of the DNA in the human genome project has given rise to a rapidly developing body of knowledge concerning genetics and to the introduction of gene therapies for an increasing number of medical conditions. The scope offered by the computer for the analysis of information and data is enormous and seemingly endless. Consequently, computer-based methods of collecting, collating, analysing, storing, and transmitting information are being applied to an increasing number of areas of economic and social activity.

Yet the codification of articulable knowledge ultimately depends upon the economic incentives to undertake the process of codification. Where knowledge is changing rapidly, leading to speedy redundancy, the benefits of codification may not be sufficient to cover the costs involved. Moreover, if codified knowledge can be easily replicated and applied in competing organizations, resistance to codification may be employed as a means to protect knowledge. In addition, as Cowan and Foray (1997) note, technological change can affect the economics of codification. For instance, the development of new languages may allow the codification of knowledge previously thought inherently tacit; or our ability to create models of phenomena and activities may be extended, perhaps with the assistance of ever-growing computing power. Furthermore, changes in the technologies of coding and decoding may improve, as may the technologies of storage, recording, and diffusion of messages. By reducing the cost and expanding the scope of codification, technological developments promote the codification of knowledge.

In the early development of knowledge management practices, the codification of knowledge was viewed as an important mechanism to spread knowledge of best practice throughout the organization, and in this way to retain knowledge when individuals left the organization. An organization cannot own its workforce, yet individuals or groups hold much organizational knowledge that is important. How can an organization secure such knowledge? It must do so either by earning the loyalty of its members or by extracting the knowledge from members and embedding it in machinery, databases, and routines. The strategy of deskilling workers can be traced back to the time and motion studies of Frederick Winslow Taylor (1911) in the late nineteenth and early twentieth centuries. By observing and analysing the flow of work, Taylor sought to identify and codify the best way to achieve a particular task and thereby improve labour productivity. In the process of applying such scientific management methods, knowledge is extracted from workers and this ensures that the best working methods are available across the whole organization. However, the bargaining position of the workforce is reduced, because the organization's managers are able to retain and deploy knowledge previously in the sole possession of its workers.

However, the codification of work processes does not always capture all the knowledge required to complete a job successfully. Julian Orr's (1996) study of photocopier repair technicians at Xerox PARC, *Talking about Machines: An Ethnography of a Modern Job*, serves to highlight the deficiencies of knowledge management strategies focused solely on codified knowledge. The Xerox technicians studied were supposed to be able to find in the company's repair manuals all the knowledge required to repair a copier machine. In the process of repairing Xerox machines, which are complex pieces of equipment that are affected by their particular environment and by the way they are used, technicians encountered problems that were not fully accounted for in the manuals. Nevertheless, they learned to overcome these problems through learning by doing and through engaging in the community of Xerox technicians during their regular breakfasts and lunches together, where they exchanged knowledge by recounting 'war stories' from the field. In this way the technicians developed knowledge in a social context, as they shared their experiences with, and learned from the experience of, other community members.

Hence it is not always possible to extract all relevant knowledge from the workforce through codification. Indeed the knowledge of some highly skilled sections of the workforce is difficult to articulate and not easily codified. Besides, if such workers are to be productive, they must have a high level of autonomy, because they handle highly idiosyncratic knowledge, which is difficult or costly to codify. The knowledge possessed by such employees can only be secured within the organization by safeguarding their loyalty. Organizations must therefore provide favourable working conditions and remuneration packages for highly skilled workers; they must also develop communities around key workers with a view to embedding their knowledge within the organization.

Knowledge management strategies focused purely on building up codified knowledge resources neglect knowledge applied in practice. That is, knowledge as an object is prioritized over knowing in practice. Nevertheless, as Orr's study of Xerox technicians demonstrates, the relationship between knowledge and knowing in practice is an important one. Certain skills cannot be gained solely from a database or manual. As the educational reformer John Dewey (1938) argued, learning occurs through practical experience and social interaction. Emphasis on one to the detriment of the other can diminish the success of efforts to manage knowledge.

Davenport, De Long, and Beers (1998) identified four objectives that generally characterize knowledge management projects: to create knowledge repositories; to improve knowledge access; to enhance the knowledge environment; and to manage knowledge as an asset. The application of technology can help in the achievement of these objectives when it is combined with the necessary human elements. Although data can be captured, processed, and disseminated through technological means, knowledge requires people to create, reveal, share, and use it. Because of this human component, a flexible, evolving structure, accompanied by an organizational climate that motivates knowledge creation, sharing, and application, is essential to any knowledge management strategy.

Despite recognition of the importance of the human dimension in knowledge management, there is a widespread drive towards codifying knowledge across the economic and social spheres of society (Roberts, 2001). Economic and technological forces are promoting this trend; and they are accompanied by political and social influences. In part, the drive towards codifying is symptomatic of the increased emphasis on accountability and on the measurement of performance in all sections of the private and public sector, which has accompanied the rise of neoliberal market economies. In a book in this series, Chris Grey (2013) explores the impact of this trend on management. Performance is very difficult to measure and assess in the predominantly service-based economy that characterizes industrialized countries. Moreover, the setting of performance targets may be quite subjective. The achievement of targets requires knowledge of performance that can be captured and codified in order to demonstrate that targets have been reached. Targets therefore become skewed towards activities where performance can be easily measured, with the consequence that areas where performance knowledge is not conducive to capture and codification are neglected. The imposition of performance targets can thus undermine performance in its wider sense. In sectors like healthcare, what counts as performance can lead to results that are incompatible with the idea of compassionate care. The case of the Mid Staffordshire hospital scandal in the United Kingdom provides an example: at a time when poor care was found to lead to the deaths of 300 patients a year, the head of the country's National Health Service, Sir David Nicholson (who subsequently resigned), is reported to have praised this hospital trust for making progress towards its targets (*The Telegraph*, 2013). Strategies that attempt to assess performance must recognize the importance of tacit knowledge and of knowing in practice and must acknowledge the inherent difficulties of measuring performance through systems that rely solely on the codification of knowledge.

Recognizing the importance of both explicit and tacit knowledge is crucial for an organization that seeks to manage and retain its knowledge advantages. A further challenge is how to prevent knowledge from leaking out (Liebeskind, 1997). Clearly, different forms of knowledge have different levels of mobility, and therefore varied potentials to permeate through the boundaries of the organization. Explicit knowledge, for example, can be disseminated beyond the boundaries of the organization in the codified form of instruction manuals, directories, blueprints, software, and so on. Tacit knowledge can move across an organization's boundaries, being embodied in individuals or groups. Codified knowledge is generally more easily replicated than tacit knowledge. For instance, a manual can be photocopied or downloaded from a company intranet at little cost. Given the ease of replication, such knowledge can be readily and widely distributed. In contrast, acquiring tacit knowledge may involve recruiting new staff or supporting existing staff to engage in periods of practice-based learning. The leakage of knowledge from the organization through the loss of staff can, to some extent, be addressed through the use of legally binding confidentiality agreements (also known as non-disclosure agreements), which restrict an employee's use and dissemination of company-owned 'confidential information'. Nevertheless, retaining knowledge can be a major challenge for organizations.

One method of protecting the company's knowledge is to stake a proprietary claim to that knowledge by securing IPRs over a specific area of knowledge (see Box 4.1 for a definition of intellectual property). The current IPR system was originally developed during the Industrial Revolution, when it was intended to reflect knowledge embedded in tangible innovations like the steam engine on the spinning jenny. The purpose of an IPR regime is to ensure that those who invest time, effort, and resources in the development of a new product or service are able to recoup their investment and enjoy a return on their effort. Importantly, an appropriate IPR system provides incentives for the development of new knowledge. However, the current system is poorly equipped to protect knowledge embedded in intangible assets or in the workforce.

Box 4.1   What is intellectual property?

The World Intellectual Property Organization defines intellectual property (IP) as:

Creations of the mind: inventions, literary and artistic works, and symbols, names, images, and designs used in commerce.

IP can be divided into two forms:

1. Industrial property, including inventions (patents), trademarks, industrial designs, and geographic indications of source; and
2. Copyright, which includes literary and artistic works such as novels, poems and plays, films, musical works, artistic works such as drawings, paintings, photographs and sculptures, and architectural designs. Rights related to copyright include those of performing artists in their performances, producers of phonograms in their recordings, and those of broadcasters in their radio and television programmes.

Source: Adapted from World Intellectual Property Organization (2013), 'What is Intellectual Property?', http://www.wipo.int/about-ip/en/index. html, accessed 13 May 2013.

Nevertheless, as the importance of knowledge to the competitiveness of firms grows, so too does the incentive to protect commercially valuable knowledge. Ownership of knowledge may be secured in a number of ways, from secrecy to copyrights, trademarks, and patents. The drive towards securing and defending IPRs in the form of patents is nowhere more evident than in the high-tech sector, where there is, for instance, an ongoing battle between Apple Inc. and Samsung Electronics over patent infringements related to their touch-screen mobile devices (Bradshaw and Mundy, 2012). Indeed Apple Inc. is not only diligent in the enforcement of its patents but also renowned for the level of secrecy it maintains over the development of new products: its employees work under tight security, which is meant to prevent the diffusion of information within the organization and beyond (Stone and Vance, 2009).

Although knowledge embodied in industrial processes and products or creative expressions can be protected by the patent system or by copyrights, for some types of knowledge assets the best form of protection is secrecy in the form of trade secrets. One of the best known trade secrets is the recipe for the soft drink Coca-Cola, which is held in a purpose-built vault in a permanent exhibit at the World of Coca-Cola in Atlanta (Stafford, 2011).

The effectiveness of the IPR system is being challenged by the increasing significance of innovations embodied in intangible assets. A growing number of services and products either require a digital component like software or are themselves entirely digital (recorded music and films fall in this category). These digital products can be easily replicated and disseminated through the Internet, enabling a new model of distribution. However, digital products and services can easily be copied and distributed illegally. There is, for example, a large number of illegal peer-to-peer file-sharing services like The Pirate Bay, founded in Sweden in 2003, through which members share copies of digital products, from films and music to books and video games. Successful efforts to prosecute in the courts those who establish such communities have led Internet service providers (ISPs) to block access to their websites and services – but with little long-term impact. For instance, even though the founders of The Pirate Bay were found guilty of facilitating the illegal downloading of copyrighted material and sentenced by the Swedish court to a year in prison and a fine of £2.8 million in 2009 (Farivar, 2012), such is the tenacity of those involved in this peer-to-peer community that new routes, or proxies, to connect to the service were rapidly developed to overcome the blocking activities of ISPs. Hence copyright infringement is difficult to police in sectors where outputs are digital.

Furthermore, the increased speed of new-knowledge creation in sectors characterized by short product cycles makes the IPR systems redundant in these areas. Competitiveness is achieved by engaging in continuous new-knowledge production rather than by protecting an existing body of knowledge. The software sector provides a good example. In order to speed up the production of new software, companies are increasingly turning to open innovation, a process whereby they work with competitors, the Open Source Software (OSS) community and user groups to develop new software products. For instance, IBM uses the OSS software Linux and has donated more than 500 software patents to the Open Software Foundation while funding Linux's development to the tune of $100 million annually (Leadbeater, 2008: 97).

Nevertheless, the IPR regime remains vital in many other sectors, including biotechnology and pharmaceuticals, where large investments are required to develop new products. In such sectors, recouping product development investments through a period of monopoly profits remains important for long-term sustainability. Therefore, despite the IPR regime's weaknesses but in line with the growing significance of knowledge as a source of competitiveness, there has been an upward trend in the scale of worldwide patenting activity. The number of patent applications grew from just over 1.05 million per annum in 1995 to more than 2.35 million in 2012; over the same period the number of patents granted increased from just over 400,000 to over 1 million (World Intellectual Property Organization, 2013: 45 and 48).

The monopoly rights awarded by the IPR system over a certain body of knowledge may prevent or postpone further creativity and innovation in the area concerned. IPRs serve to privatize and monopolize knowledge, so that its benefits are restricted to those who can afford to participate in knowledge markets. Moreover, the use of IPRs to appropriate knowledge previously available freely is a global phenomenon with major negative socioeconomic consequences. Well-known examples are the patenting of the components of traditional medicines from industrializing countries by the large pharmaceutical companies and the promotion of patented seed varieties by agri-business (Alonso, 2007; Shiva, 2007). Due to such developments, traditional medicines and seed varieties that were once available at low cost have now acquired prices that make them out of reach for the communities that originally produced them.

Moreover, the high cost of securing and protecting IPRs under the current regulatory system gives large multinational corporations (MNCs) an advantage over smaller firms in the race for knowledge commodification. As Lessig (2004) demonstrates in relation to the passage of the Sonny Bono Copyright Term Extension Act in the USA, the lobbying activities of large MNCs like the Disney Corporation have been influential in the development of IPR law. Not surprisingly, then, there is also much debate about the validity, nature, and scope of IPRs (see, for instance, Boldrin and Levine, 2008). Once knowledge is privatized through the IPR system, its use becomes restricted to those who can pay for the right to use it. As we will see in Chapter 5, the commodification of knowledge has consequences for creativity and innovation.

Methods of knowledge retention depend on the nature of the knowledge to be retained. While individuals and groups within the organization hold tacit knowledge, explicit knowledge may be held in the codified form of manuals and patents. Different types of knowledge require different forms of knowledge retention and different protection strategies. Retaining tacit knowledge requires embedding knowledge within communities and ensuring that remuneration and work conditions are conducive to the retention of key experts and of the communities within which they work. In contrast, the retention of codified knowledge may necessitate the use of legally enforceable IPRs like patents or copyrights, or the use of secrecy. The purpose of efforts to retain knowledge within the boundaries of the organization is to secure competitive advantage. However, securing competitiveness may also require the ability to transfer knowledge both within an organization and across several organizations.

Knowledge transfer

The challenges of knowledge transfer

Within the literature on knowledge management various terms are used to refer to the diffusion of knowledge from one party to another. The terms 'exchange', 'transfer', and 'sharing' knowledge are sometimes used interchangeably. In addition, scholars writing from different perspectives tend to prefer some terms over others. For instance, scholars in the field of economics may speak about knowledge exchange or transfer where scholars in organization studies are more likely to speak of knowledge sharing. 'Knowledge sharing' suggests a mutual exchange of knowledge; but at any single point in time the shared knowledge may be travelling in only one direction, while over any period of time a bidirectional flow of knowledge may occur. 'Exchange of knowledge' suggests a more formal movement of knowledge in exchange for something – perhaps other knowledge or other assets. Moreover, the term 'exchange' suggests a market transaction. 'Knowledge transfer' derives from the idea of technology transfer and may also involve a formal exchange of resources. Knowledge, like technology, may be transferred under licence for a one-off fee, for ongoing royalty payments, or in a combination of both. Hence the notion of knowledge transfer incorporates the idea of knowledge exchanged in return for some other asset (or for other knowledge). We can also talk of knowledge transfer when the process does not stimulate a return flow of resources. For this reason I adopt here the concept of 'knowledge transfer', using it to refer to all the forms that the movement of knowledge between parties can take and recognizing that knowledge transfer can occur through formal market exchanges or through informal sharing practices.

Knowledge transfer occurs when knowledge is diffused from one individual or group of individuals to others. Knowledge can be transferred through processes of socialization, education, and learning. It may be purposefully transferred, or it may occur as an outcome of other activity. Organizations and institutions have a central role in facilitating knowledge transfer. For the transfer of knowledge for commercial purposes, the relevant organizations and institutions are firms and markets, together with the legal and commercial institutional arrangements within which they operate. While firms can be viewed as repositories of knowledge, they are also active in promoting the transfer of knowledge through the activities of management and (more generally) personnel, as well as through the establishment of routines.

Knowledge may be transferred both between departments and groups *within* organizations and *beyond* the boundaries of organizations – either deliberately or surreptitiously. Some knowledge may be sticky and may flow less easily within and beyond the organization. Discussions of 'sticky knowledge' focus mainly on the challenge of moving knowledge between individuals and groups *inside* organizations. For instance, Eric von Hippel (1994) outlines the difficulty of transferring knowledge between research labs and engineering departments, while Gabriel Szulanski (1996) identifies the 'stickiness' of knowledge in efforts to circulate 'best practice' from one part of an organization to another. Additionally, where knowledge is a source of power for individuals or groups, its transfer may be impeded by the incentive to hoard it (Liebowitz, 2008).

When knowledge transfer takes place, one party acquires knowledge; therefore the entire problematic that knowledge acquisition generates is also relevant to knowledge transfer. For instance, the successful transfer of knowledge requires that the recipients have sufficient absorptive capacity. The form of the transfer will depend on the nature of the knowledge involved – that is, on whether it is tacit or explicit. The transfer of knowledge, like its acquisition, will involve learning. Tacit knowledge whose learning is time-consuming will be harder to transfer than explicit knowledge with a widely accessible code.

The transfer of knowledge through market exchange presents a number of difficulties. Chapter 1 discussed the public-good nature of much knowledge, particularly its non-rivalrous and non-excludable character. These properties influence the way in which knowledge is transferred. On the one hand, the non-rivalrous character of knowledge encourages its widespread distribution, since knowledge is a kind of resource that does not diminish in quantity when it is diffused. This idea is captured in the quotation that opens this chapter. Knowledge is like a candle in that sharing the flame to light someone else's candle does not diminish your own flame; moreover, codified knowledge is easily and rapidly replicated and spread. On the other hand, because knowledge is non-excludable, the fear of losing the advantage that new knowledge gives may discourage organizations from exposing it to others. Although the quantity of knowledge does not diminish through diffusion, if the value of knowledge lies in the organization's exclusive access to it, this value will rapidly fall as the knowledge in question is diffused beyond the boundaries of the organization.

The measurement of the transfer or 'flow' of knowledge is a difficult task. Two proxy indicators of embodied diffusion and disembodied diffusion are often used. The first involves the introduction into the production process of machinery, equipment, and components that incorporate new technology and knowledge. The second involves the transmission of knowledge, technical expertise, or technology in the form of patents, licences, or know-how. In both cases, the value of the transfer can be measured in terms of the costs involved. However, knowledge transfers also occur through the movement of personnel, the purchase of consulting services, foreign direct investment, intra-firm transfers, joint ventures, mergers, acquisitions, and cooperative research agreements. The knowledge transfer component of such activities is not always clearly distinguishable. Arguably the most important dimension of knowledge transfer is the role of people in initiating and facilitating such processes within and between organizations, through person-to-person communication. Consequently, everything that encourages or inhibits interpersonal communications affects knowledge transfer.

Trust and knowledge transfer

Knowledge transfer through market transactions presents difficulties that arise from the asymmetric distribution of the information concerning the transaction between buyer and seller. The Nobel prize-winning economist George A. Akerlof considered the problems of asymmetric information in the used-car market in his seminal paper 'The market for "lemons": quality uncertainty and the market mechanism' (Akerlof, 1970). The asymmetrical distribution of information can be exploited in markets where it is difficult for buyers to judge quality prior to purchase. An unscrupulous car salesperson may emphasize the positive aspects of a used car while neglecting to convey its weaknesses. Once the buyer has purchased the car, the weaknesses will become apparent through use and the buyer may find that they have bought a 'lemon'. Problems of asymmetric information also arise in markets for knowledge, because assessing its value requires access to it, which can only be achieved once the knowledge has been purchased and absorbed. Hence, trust in the knowledge provider is required. Trust may be gained through repeated transactions – in other words it is built gradually, on the basis of experience, or it is supported through formal institutional structures. So, for instance, students taking a programme in knowledge management do not know its value until they have completed it. They may feel that the programme is of little value while they take it; and sometimes they do not see any benefits until much later, when they come to use the knowledge gained in that programme. Students put their trust in the reputation of the professors who teach them – whose knowledge is based on formal qualifications and research expertise – and in the standing of the department and institution in which they study.

National and global university league tables like the *Times Higher Education* World University Rankings, international accreditation systems like the European Quality Improvement System (EQUIS) for business schools, and reports from national bodies like the United Kingdom's Quality Assurance Agency for Higher Education help students to determine the reputation of universities and of their various departments.

While indicators of the quality of knowledge exist in sectors such as education and medicine, this is not the case in all fields. In some areas the difficulty in appreciating the value of knowledge hinders the latter's efficient allocation through the market. Market failures in the transaction of knowledge provide a rationale for vertical integration. Yet knowledge is often developed interactively and transferred through networks within and beyond the boundaries of the organization. Networks offer an important means through which knowledge may be transferred and produced; and this represents an alternative to the traditional markets–hierarchy dichotomy. Networks are increasingly recognized as important entities for the development and circulation of knowledge. Where networks exist outside the organization, they depend on self-regulation through social capital, which includes trust and reputation.

Through codification and the appropriate contractual arrangements, explicit knowledge may be transferred in a tangible embodiment such as blueprints or patents, in machinery, as part of licensing or franchise agreements, or in trade between agents. But tacit knowledge often requires considerable time to be acquired through learning by doing. As noted in Chapter 3, because knowledge is often made up of both tacit and codified elements, codified knowledge alone may fail to facilitate the successful transfer of knowledge. Hence there are elements of knowledge that can only be transferred successfully through a process of demonstration, which is facilitated by face-to-face contact between the transmitter and receiver. Harry Collins' (2001) research on the measurement of the quality factor in sapphire confirmed not only the importance of demonstration in the process of knowledge transfer, but also the significance of trust – which is evident in the personal relationships between the scientists studied.

As Francis Fukuyama (1995) has argued, the level of trust between individuals, among organizations, and within society as a whole influences the nature of economic activity in terms of the character of organizational structures and the degree of economic prosperity. Trust influences the level of risk and uncertainty arising from the transaction of commodities within organizations and in the market. Although trust is a valuable commodity, it cannot be acquired in the market because, as Arrow notes, 'if you have to buy it, you already have some doubts about what you've bought' (1974: 23). Although a rather elusive concept, trust is highly important for the efficient operation of a knowledge-based economy, since the market exchange of knowledge gives rise to a high level of risk and uncertainty. These risks and uncertainties are reduced by the presence of a high level of trust.

Taking a strictly rational approach, Casson defines trust as 'a warranted belief that someone else will honour their obligations, not merely because of material incentives, but out of moral commitment too. It is assumed that such moral commitment is rational because it generates emotional rewards' (1997: 118). More broadly, Lazaric and Lorenz (1998: 3) argue that three conditions are common in definitions of trust and, together, provide a basis for a general definition. First, trust is to be identified with an agent's belief rather than with their behaviour or action. Second, trust is to do with beliefs about the likely behaviour of another (or others) who matter for the decision-making process of the person who holds those beliefs. Finally, trust pertains to situations where the complexity of the relationship, or the fact that it is marked by unanticipated contingencies, precludes having recourse to complete contracts with third-party enforcement. Clearly the market exchange of knowledge – particularly tacit knowledge – is not always amenable to enforcement by contract; hence the importance of trust in the transfer of knowledge.

Importantly, trust is influenced by the social context; and the levels of trust present in the economic environment vary between cultures and nations. This is of particular importance to cross-border knowledge transfer, whether in the market or within the boundaries of the firm. If shared expectations are to be built, the development of trust between agents from different cultural or national backgrounds will necessitate a higher investment than the development of trust between agents who share a common background. High levels of face-to-face contact and a process of socialization are usually required to establish and reinforce a relationship of trust and confidence between agents. Furthermore, the richness of face-to-face contact can help counterbalance the communication difficulties that may arise from differences in culture and language.

Over time, an agent engaged in the market transfer of knowledge will develop an appreciation of their trading partner's social context. Together, the two will establish their own social norms and mutual expectations, thereby enabling the development of trust and, with it, successful knowledge transfer. The presence of a relationship of trust between individuals indicates the capacity for a high degree of mutual understanding, built upon a common appreciation of the social and cultural context. Both trust and mutual understanding, developed in their social and cultural contexts, are prerequisites for the successful transfer of tacit knowledge. The use of technologically mediated communication and knowledge transfer will be more successful between agents who share social, cultural, and linguistic characteristics (Roberts, 2000). It will be less effective when agents are from diverse backgrounds, particularly in the early stages of interaction, before mutually determined norms and practices have been established.

Technology and knowledge transfer

ICTs facilitate knowledge transfer through the exchange of data. Where knowledge can be codified, it can, with the use of ICTs, be distributed worldwide at the touch of a button, with little cost. But the transfer of tacit knowledge cannot be executed in such a simple fashion, since the transformation of knowledge into information and then into data will be incomplete. As a result, the transfer of tacit knowledge often requires proximity between the transmitter and receiver. The growing set of technologies of communication detailed in Table 4.1, which include videoconferencing and virtual project rooms, may aid the transfer of tacit knowledge. Nevertheless, technologically facilitated communication cannot yet replace direct face-to-face contact, which is often a prerequisite for the successful transfer of tacit knowledge. Moreover, given the importance of tacit knowledge as a factor that enables the assimilation of codified knowledge, face-to-face contact may well be a prerequisite for the transfer of much codified knowledge too. Finally, the need to establish a level of trust that can facilitate the transfer of knowledge also favours co-presence and co-location (Roberts, 2003).

Studies of the use of ICTs in the work of dispersed R&D teams, in which the transfer of knowledge and shared learning is vital, attest to the importance of face-to-face interaction. As Boutellier et al. (1998) note, sensory information, feelings, intuition, non-verbal communication, and context are largely neglected in communication facilitated through ICTs; this is due to a lack of person-to-person contact. Nevertheless, relational proximity, achieved through face-to-face interaction, can also be realized through a combination of technology-mediated communication and mobility of individuals (Coe and Bunnell, 2003). In some cases, a combination of occasional face-to-face encounters and technology-mediated communication may facilitate the development of a more trusting relationship with someone located on the other side of the world than with someone in the office next door.

Table 4.1   Examples of ICT services enabling information and knowledge transfer

ICT services	Comments
Electronic mail (e-mail)	For day-to-day project communication and the transfer of documents (including minutes and agendas of meetings, project reports, schedules, images, etc.).
SMS	A text messaging service component of phone, web, or mobile communication systems, which allows the exchange of short text messages between devices.
Instant messaging services	Microsoft's MSN Messenger.
Voice mail	Asynchronous audio communication.
Teleconferencing	Telephone discussions between more than two people.
Videoconferencing	Group meeting among geographically dispersed individuals (often formal). Videoconference rooms may be dedicated to particular projects, allowing for frequent use. Includes the use of the freely available Skype service as well as commercially provided systems.
Desktop videoconferencing	One-to-one meeting, or in small groups (often informal). May include shared computer displays and virtual project rooms.
CAD and CAM	For the transmission of specifications from design to manufacturing.
Discussion lists	Information can be shared and stored through questions and answers, knowledge that would otherwise remain solely with individual members of the organization.
Blogs	Single-authored or multi-authored informational sites published on the World Wide Web and consisting of discrete entries or 'posts', normally displayed in reverse chronological order. Many blogs use the open-source blogging platform WordPress.
Information databases	For common access to project data.

(Continued)

Table 4.1   (Continued)

ICT services	Comments
Shared drives on corporate networks and commercial file-hosting services	All manner of digital content can be shared through joint access to computer drives and folders within organizational specific Intranets, as well as through externally provided file-sharing services such as Dropbox.
Social media	Interactions among people in which they create, share, and exchange information, ideas, and multimedia content in virtual communities and networks (e.g. Facebook, Twitter, Instagram, Tumblr and Flickr). Allow quick communication between group members.
Websites hosting FAQ pages	Frequently asked questions and answers are captured and made widely accessible.
Wikis	A website that allows people to add, modify, or delete content via a web browser. Wikis use specialized wiki software and are usually created collaboratively (e.g. Wikipedia).
Virtual worlds	Computer-based simulated environment contexts in which interlocutors can engage in rich multidimensional communication (e.g. Second Life).
Groupware	Includes a range of the facilities listed above. Examples include IBM Notes and Domino (formerly Lotus Notes) and Microsoft Exchange and Novell GroupWise.

ICTs are becoming increasingly sophisticated and, in certain circumstances where the individuals involved in the transaction are highly attuned to their use, they may facilitate or support the transfer of tacit knowledge. For instance, members of the OSS community are engaged in developing and transferring knowledge as part of their activity. They are especially familiar with the use of ICTs and they work on codes that exist in abstract form. They engage in knowing in practice as they compose and revise code online. Hence they have a specialized knowledge of knowing code in practice, even though their work is always mediated through ICTs. Software programmers develop a shared aesthetic appreciation of the code they work with; for example, they commonly refer to code as elegant or beautiful (Oram and Wilson, 2007).

Programmers working together at a distance can share knowledge through an understanding of the elegance or beauty of the code in the same way in which the flute-makers studied by Cook and Yanow (1993) shared knowledge through the feel of the tangible instruments they co-produced.

This suggests that tacit knowledge can be transformed into information, which, when converted into data, may be transferred across distance electronically. However, this tacit-to-tacit knowledge transfer arises from the transfer of codified knowledge, which, when combined with the tacit knowledge of the receiver, gives rise to *new* tacit knowledge (Roberts, 2000). Tacit knowledge can then emerge from the assimilation and absorption of codified knowledge. In this way ICTs can enhance the transfer of knowledge by supporting the creation of tacit knowledge. ICTs increase the sharing of information and of information about sources of knowledge, as well as the sharing of knowledge about sources of information. However, in most cases ICTs alone fail to capture fully the conditions required for the successful transfer of tacit knowledge. Two individuals on different sides of the world can read the same codified knowledge embedded in a document delivered to them simultaneously through e-mail. However, these individuals cannot share tacit knowledge effectively, not even with the help of desktop videoconferencing, unless they are in a common social and cultural context. If this condition is fulfilled, they may *share* tacit knowledge by assimilating codified knowledge and thereby creating new tacit knowledge that will be largely – though not completely – the same. Indeed, if Michael Polanyi's (1958) view of knowledge as fundamentally centred on the individual is accepted, it is questionable whether individuals can share their tacit knowledge base in its entirety. The most that can be achieved is a high degree of overlap between the tacit knowledge held by persons who work together in a group.

Shared cultural expectations and beliefs about the behaviour and actions of others provide the basis on which to build a relationship of trust and mutual understanding. For ICTs to assist knowledge transfer across distance, the individuals involved must succeed in creating a virtual location in which they share a social and cultural–institutional framework. In a sense, co-presence is facilitated through a combination of ICTs and shared social and cultural understanding. Only then can technologically assisted methods of communication be used to optimum effect. The need to fulfil this prerequisite restricts the scope of technologically assisted communication as a replacement for face-to-face contact. Such communication may be a useful complementary device designed to reinforce communications achieved through face-to-face contact. However, face-to-face contact remains a vital element in the establishment of a relationship of trust, which is an important condition for the efficient transfer of knowledge – both in the market and within organizations.

Conclusion

This chapter has highlighted the human element needed in the acquisition, retention, and transfer of knowledge. Although explicit knowledge can be transferred in a codified form independently of humans, if organizations are to absorb and apply such knowledge, people must interpret it. Moreover, explicit and tacit knowledge are interdependent in the sense that codified knowledge must be interpreted with the help of tacit knowledge, and in the process of interpreting codified knowledge new tacit knowledge is created. The acquisition, retention, and transfer of knowledge involve creative processes, which will be examined in the next chapter.

An important lesson to take from this chapter is that the management of knowledge requires paying attention to both its explicit and its tacit dimensions. One without the other will lead to the inefficient and ineffective management of one of the most valuable resources that organizations hold. Managers must balance the desire to capture and codify knowledge against the need to recognize and retain tacit knowledge within the organization. Given the tacit forms of knowledge and knowing in practice, the challenge of managing knowledge becomes one of managing the workforce in an appropriate fashion. Moreover, the acquisition and transfer of knowledge depend upon interaction between people. Communication is much more than codified signals: it is complex and subtle. It is not possible to take people and their need for trust and mutual understanding out of the knowledge management equation. This is because knowledge is acquired, retained, transferred, and applied in a social context.

Note

1. Visit the site at www.dunnhumby.com/uk/what-we-do (accessed 13 July 2014).

5

Knowledge, Creativity, and Innovation

Science is organized knowledge.

Herbert Spencer

Knowledge acquisition through creativity and innovation is the focus of this chapter. In order to explore the relationship between these three entities, we need to look more closely at what we mean by creativity and innovation. It will then be possible to assess how knowledge management can contribute to the creative process, and therefore to innovation.

The terms 'creativity' and 'innovation' are often used interchangeably, and increasingly so. Although I follow this practice, I will also point to an important distinction between what they designate. Therefore the chapter begins by considering what creativity is and how it relates to innovation. Then it turns to the topic of organizing knowledge for creativity and innovation; here particular attention is given to how innovative activity has evolved since the late twentieth century. This is followed by an examination of the notion of the knowledge-creating company, as elaborated by Nonaka and Takeuchi. The chapter ends by investigating the role of the community in facilitating knowledge acquisition through creativity and innovation.

Creativity and innovation

In the knowledge economy, creativity and innovation are essential for success in markets that are characterized by intense competition. In these markets the speed of innovation and the capacity for continual creativity have become subjects of popular interest, as evidenced by the publication of numerous books and reports on the creative economy and its various components in the first decade of the twenty-first century. Examples include John Howkins' (2002) *The Creative Economy* and Richard Florida's (2002) *The Rise of the Creative Class*. The adoption of the idea of the creative economy by national and international policymakers suggests that we are witnessing a shift from the rhetoric of the knowledge economy to the idea of a creative economy.

Industrialized and industrializing countries alike see the creative industries as a source of economic growth. For instance, the UK government was among the first to map the creative industries (Department of Culture, Media and Sport, 1998) with a view to promoting this area of increasing economic importance. At an international level, the United Nations produces regular reports on the creative economy that focus on the potential for development through the creative industries (United Nations, 2008, 2010, 2013).

Such initiatives help to identify and classify the creative industries as well as the creative potential of particular locations. For example, Florida (2002) provides us with a Creativity Index. This is a composite measure based on four equally weighted indices: the creative class share of the workforce; the High-Tech Index – based on the Milken Institute's widely accepted Tech Pole Index; innovation, measured as patents per capita; and diversity, measured by the Gay Index – a proxy for openness. This Creativity Index provides a means of assessing the potential creativity of particular locations: the higher its value the greater the propensity for creativity. Yet, despite studies of this sort, the source of creativity remains elusive.

Much attention has been devoted to understanding the characteristics of creative individuals. For instance, in a 2014 special edition of *Scientific American Mind* focused on creativity, all but 2 of the 17 articles concentrated on individual creativity. Perhaps not surprisingly for a publication dedicated to the mind, the papers in the special issue reflect common views according to which creativity is largely the outcome of individual behaviour and often results from some innate and/or nurtured genius. Indeed, the identification of the characteristics of creative people has attracted much research attention. For instance, in her theory of creativity, Teresa Amabile (1997) of the Harvard Business School identifies three key components of individual creativity: expertise, creative-thinking skills, and intrinsic task motivation. She argues that creativity is most likely to occur when an individual's skills overlap with their strongest intrinsic interests; and the higher the level of each of these three elements, the greater the propensity for creativity. Meanwhile, the psychologist Mihaly Csikszentmihalyi (1996) focuses on the personal qualities of creative people. From a study of 91 eminent people, he identifies the following 10 antithetical traits often present in creative people:

1. They have a great deal of physical energy, but they are also often quiet and at rest.
2. They tend to be smart yet naive at the same time.
3. They combine playfulness and discipline, or responsibility and irresponsibility.

4. They alternate between displaying either imagination and fantasy or a rooted sense of reality.
5. They tend to be both extrovert and introvert.
6. They are humble and proud at the same time.
7. To an extent, they escape rigid gender-role stereotyping.
8. They are both rebellious and conservative.
9. Most are very passionate about their work, yet they can be extremely objective about it as well.
10. Their openness and sensitivity often expose them to suffering and pain, yet also give them a great deal of enjoyment.

As Chris Bilton (2007) argues in his *Management and Creativity*, this focus on the individual as a source of creativity is evident in popular and management debates, which emphasize the role of creative individuals and their need for freedom in expressing their talent or vision. This conception is reflected in reports on how companies noted for their creativity, like Google, Lego, Pixar, and Sony, provide opportunities for individual creativity and play in the workplace in the form of recreational areas replete with brightly coloured beanbags, games, and other forms of entertainment. The link between individualism and creativity is rooted in the western philosophical tradition. Yet Bilton (2007) goes on to argue that conflating creativity with individualism disconnects creative thinking and creative people from the sociocultural and economic contexts that give meaning and value to innovations and individual talents. Moreover, Csikszentmihalyi notes that

> creativity results from the interaction of a system composed of three elements: a culture that contains symbolic rules, a person who brings novelty into the symbolic domain, and a field of experts who recognize and validate the innovation. All three are necessary for a creative idea, product, or discovery to take place. (1996: 6)

Nevertheless, the stereotype of the lone inventor obsessed with the development of some product who then makes a major breakthrough by chance, in a *eureka* moment, remains a common feature in popular accounts of creativity. This type of narrative characterizes the story of the discovery of penicillin by Alexander Fleming. Known as a brilliant though untidy researcher, Fleming was investigating a strain of bacteria called staphylococci. In the summer of 1928 he went on holiday leaving a stack of cultures of staphylococci on a bench in the corner of his laboratory. On return, he noticed that one culture had been contaminated with a fungus. While the colonies of staphylococci that had immediately surrounded the fungus had been destroyed, others that were farther away were unaffected. After investigating this fungus, Fleming discovered its origins and in March 1929 named the substance 'penicillin'. This is often where the story ends – with a lone inventor and a dose of serendipity having led to a major breakthrough in the treatment of bacterial infections. However, it is important to note that although Fleming published his findings in 1929, it was not until the 1940s that Howard Florey and Ernst Boris Chain developed a process of mass production of penicillin for the successful treatment of bacterial infections. In recognition of their work on penicillin, Fleming, Florey, and Chain jointly received the Nobel Prize in Medicine in 1945. In reality, the creation of a useful product is often the outcome of the coordinated activities of many contributors.

Furthermore, the level of originality required for something to be creative or innovative is debatable. In his seminal book on the *Diffusion of Innovations*, Everett Rogers defined innovation as

> an idea, practice, or object that is perceived as new by an individual or other unit of adoption. It matters little, so far as human behavior is concerned, whether or not an idea is 'objectively' new as measured by the lapse of time since its first use or discovery. The perceived newness of the idea for the individual determines his or her reaction to it. If the idea seems new to the individual, it is an innovation. Newness in an innovation need not just involve new knowledge. Someone may have known about an innovation for some time but not yet developed a favorable or unfavorable attitude toward it, nor have adopted or rejected it. The 'newness' aspect of an innovation may be expressed in terms of knowledge, persuasion, or a decision to adopt. (1962: 11)

For Rogers, then, an innovation is an idea or practice that is new to the individual. Yet Margaret Boden (2004: 2) makes an important distinction between innovations that are new to the individual, which she subsumes to psychological creativity (P-creativity), and innovations that are new to the world, which she puts down to historical creativity (H-creativity). Clearly, for an innovation to have value in the business context, it must be new to the world – in the sense that it should deviate in some way from established business norms and conventions – rather than merely new to the individual (Bilton, 2007: 3). Moreover, Amabile notes that in the field of business, creativity goes beyond originality: 'To be creative, an idea must also be appropriate – useful and actionable. It must somehow influence the way business gets done – by improving a product, for instance, or by opening up a new way to approach a process' (1998: 78).

It is instructive to consider how an innovation is defined in relation to intellectual property rights (IPRs). To meet the criteria required to secure patent protection, an innovation must represent a significant 'inventive step' beyond what is already known. Moreover, it must be more than abstract knowledge: it must make possible a new application in practice. Similarly, for copyright protection, an idea must be a deliberate result of individual skill, not an accidental discovery, and it must be expressed in concrete, tangible form (Bilton, 2007: 3). You may be highly creative, developing new ideas daily; but if you just keep these ideas in your head, they cannot be protected as your property. For creativity to be recognized in the IPR system, it must be made explicit and thereby externalized and separated from the creator.

It is useful at this point to highlight the distinction between creativity and innovation, a distinction that has become increasingly blurred in the last decade or so with the rising amount of attention given to creativity. Although creativity is a necessary component in innovation, it alone does not guarantee innovation. From an economic perspective, innovation involves the development of some new knowledge or invention that can result in intermediate and/or final products and services available in commercial markets. Innovation, then, necessitates the development of value from creativity and invention. So, although in contemporary discussions the concepts of creativity and innovation are often conflated, it is important to recognize that they also have distinct meanings. Nevertheless, to take an invention through to the market may require a degree of creative thinking at every stage in the process, from the generation of a new idea through to the manufacturing of the corresponding object, its delivery system, its marketing and sales, and even the consumption process.

Organizing knowledge for creativity and innovation

Scholars of creativity have identified a range of organizational conditions that stimulate creativity. For instance, Amabile (1997, 1998) argues that creativity at an organizational level requires organizational motivation to innovate, resources to facilitate creativity, and appropriate management practices that encourage and support creative activity. Management practices should seek to harness and channel the creativity of individuals. Existing knowledge and the expertise held by an organization are important resources required for creativity, as is an organization's capacity to learn from and build upon existing knowledge, both within and beyond its own boundaries. Creative individuals usually recognize that their own creativity draws on the knowledge developed by others, as Isaac Newton, the seventeenth-century English scientist, noted: 'If I have seen further it is by standing on the shoulders of Giants' (Turnbull, 1959: 416). Hence the organization of knowledge through knowledge management strategies has a key role in facilitating the development of creativity.

James G. March (1991: 71) highlights an important distinction between exploitative and exploratory innovation. Through the exploitation of existing knowledge in new situations or applications, incremental innovations can be achieved. For example, when Nestlé, the producer of the four-fingered chocolate-covered wafer biscuit KitKat, introduces new varieties of KitKat (like the Pop Choc and KitKat Chunky versions) as well as different flavours, this can be seen as incremental innovation. Through exploration for new knowledge with the aim of developing novel products or processes, radical innovations can result. In relation to chocolate biscuits, a radical innovation might take the form of a low-calorie or fat-free product that gives the same satisfaction as the existing chocolate biscuit bars, which are high in calories and rich in fat. Wishful thinking perhaps? The development of such a product would require exploration for new knowledge rather than applying existing knowledge to produce slight variations on existing products. To be successful in the long term, organizations need to engage in both incremental innovation through the exploitation of existing knowledge and radical innovation through the exploration for new knowledge.

Organizing knowledge for creativity is a difficult task, for creativity may depend on spontaneity and serendipity – factors that cannot be rationalized or engineered. However, some types of innovation depend on search, experimentation, and testing techniques that can be rationalized and conducted in a highly systematic manner. For instance, Josiah Wedgewood's development, in the eighteenth century, of the matt-finished coloured pottery known as jasperware, for which his company remains known today, depended upon many hundreds of methodically conducted scientific experiments designed to achieve the required quality of colour. Likewise, the mapping of the human genome – the results of which have opened vast opportunities for innovative products and processes, all based on the manipulation of genes – was achieved through a laborious repetitive computer-aided process of decoding the DNA that underlies all living entities. This demonstrates that innovation requires not only creative thought, but also persistence and patience in tracing, tracking, and identifying components. These activities can be rationalized, for example, in the large research and development (R&D) laboratories of private and public sector research centres.

The twentieth century saw the rise of large corporations with extensive R&D departments. However, by the 1970s, economic conditions had caused corporate restructuring and downsizing, as businesses moved to more flexible organizational forms. Within large corporations, this process often led to the externalization of departments and activities that could be better undertaken by specialist organizations. While R&D activity remains important for knowledge-intensive products, there is increasing scope for the externalization of repetitive testing activities, which are outsourced to independent R&D laboratories.

At the same time, the nature of the innovations and the speed of changes required corporations to look beyond their boundaries and to identify knowledge opportunities available among small start-up companies and university spin-offs, in fields such as biotechnology and software development. No individual company can be sure of staying ahead of the competition; hence alliances with competitors, joint ventures, mergers and acquisitions, technical agreements, and all manner of creative management strategies are required to sustain a steady flow of new products and processes. For instance, in the automobile sector strategic alliances involving the development of jointly produced car platforms are common. The global strategic alliance announced in February 2012 between PSA Peugeot Citroën and General Motors is typical and involves the sharing of knowledge in engineering development and design. Similarly, in 2014 global technology giants Apple and IBM announced a partnership in which they would develop their business software by pooling their expertise and resources in mobile computing.

Collaboration also occurs through the activities of staff beyond the boundaries of the firm. Knowledge workers engage in external associations and communities in which they develop their knowledge independently of their employer, and the knowledge they acquire there may be applied in the organization. Moreover, organizations are increasingly engaging in open-innovation initiatives (Chesbrough, 2006); for example, as noted in Chapter 4, IBM has begun to invest in open-source platforms such as Linux, thereby reducing its server software production costs.

For a number of reasons, the nature of commercial innovative activity has become increasingly diverse since the late twentieth century. First, service activity has grown significantly as a proportion of total economic activity over the past 50 years, and the nature of innovation in services tends to be based on the development of new forms of delivery and organization rather than on the development of new products. The repetitive testing and searching for new components gives way to market research and delivery design, which require different skills and research resources.

Second, the revolution in information and communications technology (ICT) has both accelerated the rate of innovation and extended its range – opening up new areas, such as those related to mobile telephones and digital media. The power of computers and digital technologies to collect, search, collate, analyse, and disseminate information is transforming the scale and speed of innovation and new-knowledge creation. Much new knowledge results from recombining existing knowledge in new ways. The ICT revolution has increased the amount and the availability of knowledge and information, as well as the ease with which they may be analysed, thereby increasing the scope for creativity through recombination.

Third, the lower cost of sophisticated digital technologies allows for the production of innovation on a small scale. This is particularly the case when the output is a service that can be delivered via the Internet. For instance, the teenager Nick D'Aloiso created the news-summarizing app Summly while revising for his school exams in 2011; it sold to Yahoo for £20 million in 2013 (Rainey, 2013). Furthermore, the declining cost of 3D printers is revolutionizing the capacity of small organizations to engage in the development of tangible products. The huge resources of large corporations are not always necessary for the development of new services, products, or processes.

Fourth, the Internet and mobile communications have empowered consumers to engage in innovative activity in terms of the way they use new products and services or communicate with producers in the development of new goods and services. As Eric von Hippel (2005) argues, we are witnessing a democratization of innovation in relation to the activities of lead-users, and this process facilitates the development of new products and services in collaboration with commercial providers or Open Source Software (OSS) communities. For instance, businesses from IBM to Nokia are actively engaging with lead-user and OSS communities to support their own innovation activities.

A fifth reason for the changing nature of innovation is supplied by globalization, which has given rise to viable niche markets for which innovative efforts were not previously profitable. The niche market, which Chris Anderson (2008) calls 'the long tail' (in an eponymous book dedicated to this phenomenon), can be reached through the Internet and social media platforms. When niche markets are aggregated across the globe, they become large profitable markets. Therefore there is now an incentive to innovate for the niche market.

Sixth, the ability to access existing knowledge has increased through globalization, higher levels of education, and the development of databases and textual resources available freely or at low cost, via the Internet, to increasing numbers of people. Free sources of knowledge range from the online encyclopaedia Wikipedia to university-level programmes such as the Massachusetts Institute of Technology (MIT)'s OpenCourseWare. With such resources at hand, the incremental knowledge advances achieved by individuals and organizations have a greatly enhanced potential of growing into radical innovations. Moreover, the Internet, mobile communications, and social media have revolutionized the speed with which information can circulate among globe-spanning real and virtual communities. These technologies, together with the distance that people travel for work and pleasure, have dramatically extended the mobility of information and knowledge, and therefore the scope to leverage such resources for innovation.

The seventh point is related to the rise of 'big data'. Big data are vast data sets that result from the automatic collection of data in today's digitally connected world. Combined with the extraordinary computing power that is currently available, big data have a huge potential for the development of new knowledge. In their recent book *Big Data*, Viktor Mayer-Schönberger and Kenneth Cukier (2013) describe how the data collected by Google can be used to track the spread of the flu virus. While traditional methods of tracking disease involve the collection of data through doctors who reported cases to the medical authorities, Google is able to trace the diffusion of the flu virus by analysing a vast body of current data concerning the frequency with which flu-related terms are entered into its search engine together with the location of those undertaking the searches for flu-related information. When the H1N1 virus struck in 2009, Google's analysis proved to be a more useful and timely indicator than government statistics, which suffered from a reporting lag. The understanding gained from the analysis of huge data sets can be usefully employed in the production of new knowledge.

Finally, in the contemporary world there is huge potential for different cultural and knowledge communities to interact. The dissonance that arises from bringing together difference can be highly creative. For example, the frictions between groups of different experts can give rise to new insights. Cross-disciplinary work can be highly creative and lead to knowledge breakthroughs that would not be possible from within one discipline. It is for this reason that governments and related bodies support interactions between art and science. For instance, the Centre for Research in Art and Science in the Humanities at Curtin University, sponsored by the Australian Technology Network of Universities, seeks to bring art and science together to produce new knowledge.[1] However, if different communities are to work together productively, there must be sufficient cognitive proximity for those involved to communicate effectively (Nooteboom, 2009).

Innovation in different sectors requires different types of organization. The level of organization depends on the extent to which innovative activity needs the coordination of tangible resources and on the scale of these resources. As the examples detailed below illustrate, where tangible resources are extensive, a more formal and complex organizational structure is necessary than where the resources are on a smaller scale or are intangible in nature.

CERN, the European Organization for Nuclear Research, brings together physicists and engineers from 21 member countries to explore the fundamental structure of the universe. With a permanent staff of 2,500 and a constant influx of around 10,000 visiting experts, CERN manages some of the world's largest and most complex scientific instruments, namely those required in the study of the most basic constituents of matter.[2] One such piece of equipment is the 27-kilometre Large Hadron Collider, which accelerates and collides protons at energies approaching the speed of light. This machine, which cost about €3 billion, is dependent on the sponsorship of the various partner states. The workforces at CERN hold crucial intangible knowledge and experience that, when combined with the tangible resources, facilitate the production of new knowledge aimed at explaining the very fundamentals of life. While the intangible resources held by the workforce are mobile and can be dispersed across the globe, the tangible resources are centralized at the CERN particle physics laboratory in Switzerland. The operation and success of the laboratory depends on its formal hierarchical organizational structure.

A rather different example is that of the production of software organized through the OSS community. Here the tangible resources required for participation – a laptop and an Internet connection – are extremely small by comparison with those required in the field of particle physics. Laptops and Internet connections are available to the many thousands of OSS community members spread across the globe, who contribute their time on a voluntary basis. The key resource required in the production of software is the knowledge of participating programmers. The characteristics of the OSS community are evident in other knowledge-producing communities. In his book *The Wealth of Networks*, Yochai Benkler (2006) documents the activity of a range of other online communities engaged in the production of knowledge: NASA Clickworkers, which is concerned with tracking craters on Mars; Project Gutenburg, which involves the scanning of books so that they become freely available in digital form; SETI@home, which helps in the search for extraterrestrial life; and Fightaids@home, which supports the search for drugs to fight HIV/AIDS. What Benkler shows is that the combined efforts of individuals who make small contributions to large-scale projects can give rise to important advancements in knowledge. Yet, given the distributed nature of the tangible and intangible resources required, the organization of such activity occurs through an informal community rather than through a formal hierarchical organizational structure.

This shows that knowledge creation and innovation can occur in formal organizational structures or in informal, community-type configurations. In the knowledge management literature, two of the most popular approaches to understanding knowledge generation – which are based on Nonaka and Takeuchi (1995) and Lave and Wenger (1991) – describe creativity and innovation as occurring in these two distinct forms. The formal organization is evident in the notion of the knowledge-creating company; and the informal community is manifest in the idea of communities of practice. The remainder of this chapter explores these two approaches to understanding the generation of knowledge.

The knowledge-creating company

Ikujiro Nonaka and Hirotaka Takeuchi's (1995) *The Knowledge-Creating Company* is one of the most highly cited books in the field of knowledge management. To produce their theory of knowledge creation, the authors synthesized an understanding of the role of knowledge in the organization and in the process of innovation. Moreover, they identify two dimensions of knowledge creation – epistemological and ontological. The ontological dimension recognizes the primary import of the individual in the creation of knowledge. The organization supports creativity in individuals by providing an appropriate context. For Nonaka and Takeuchi, organizational knowledge creation involves a process that amplifies the knowledge created by individuals. This process occurs in a 'community of interaction' across the organization and even reaches beyond its boundaries. The theory has elements of a practice-based approach in the sense that knowledge, which is defined as justified true belief, is viewed as centred on the individual and relates to human values and ideas. However, Nonaka and Takeuchi draw on Polanyi's (1966) distinction between tacit and explicit knowledge for their epistemological dimension, thereby viewing explicit knowledge as separable from the individual; and this gives an objectivist dimension to their model. At the same time their approach is influenced by the Japanese intellectual tradition, which emphasizes oneness of body and mind, oneness of self and other, and oneness of humanity and nature. This contrasts with western rationalist approaches to knowledge which, influenced by the Cartesian duality of body and mind, focus on the individual and on the separation of knowledge from the world through abstract thought.

At the centre of Nonaka and Takeuchi's theory of organizational knowledge creation is the interaction between tacit and explicit knowledge. As knowledge moves beyond the individual through a process of *socialization* (S), tacit knowledge is *externalized* (E) and thus becomes able to move between members of the organization. Moreover, once articulated, knowledge can be codified and embedded in texts and artefacts. Such forms of explicit knowledge are *combined* (C) with the knowledge already held by individuals, and, as part of the process, they are also *internalized* (I). Through the internalization process new tacit knowledge is created, which is distinct from the original tacit knowledge. For Nonaka and Takeuchi, creativity occurs in this cycle of socialization, externalization, combination, and internalization: it occurs within individuals, and thereby within the firm. As knowledge moves through these stages, it oscillates between tacit and explicit forms; it passes from one mode to another in a continuous cycle, generating a spiral of organizational knowledge creation. This is a model of knowledge conversion, and it is commonly known as the SECI model (Figure 5.1).

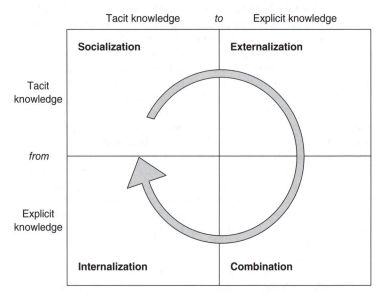

Figure 5.1   SECI Model: From four modes of conversion to the knowledge spiral

Source: Developed from Nonaka and Takeuchi (1995: 62 and 71).

Nonaka and Takeuchi illustrate their model of knowledge conversion through the example of the Japanese company Matsushita Electric Industrial Co. Ltd's development of the home bakery machine – the first fully automatic bread-making machine for home use, introduced on the Japanese market in 1987. The case illustrates how knowledge moves between the four stages of socialization, externalization, combination, and internalization within organizations. Innovations like the home bakery machine require several iterations of the knowledge-creating cycle; they also require supportive organizational conditions. An account of how the process moves through one of its cycles shows how individual tacit knowledge is shared and made explicit before being transformed through combination.

For example, the project team developing the home bakery machine had to address the problem of making a machine that kneads dough correctly. Although the process of kneading dough may look quite straightforward, skill is involved in performing the optimal combination of movements that can maximize the effectiveness of this process. A skilled baker will have an intimate understanding of how to combine the ingredients and of how the feel of the dough changes as the dough progresses through kneading. Such knowledge is tacit and acquired through learning by doing. The movements that make up the process look simple; yet, if you have ever tried to make bread, you will know that the results of a novice are unlikely to match those of a master baker. Some years ago, for a short period of time, I took up making bread without the help of a bread-making machine. Although the kneading process was a great stress reliever, the results of my work were rarely consistent, often rather stodgy, and even though I enjoyed eating my own home-made bread, I would not have won any prizes for quality.

To gain the skills of a master baker, it is necessary to become an apprentice and work alongside a baker. Therefore, in order to embed the skills of a master baker into a machine – that is, in order to externalize them for incorporation into mechanical actions – one had to acquire them first, through learning. To achieve this, Ikuko Tanaka, a member of the project-developing team, worked as an apprentice to the head baker at the Osaka International Hotel. Through *socialization* she observed and imitated the head baker; in this process tacit knowledge was shared through the development of common mental models, language, and social practices. Tanaka then engaged in a process of *externalization* by articulating and translating tacit knowledge into explicit concepts; for instance, she employed the phrase 'twisting and stretching' to capture the kneading process; and she also communicated the speed of such actions when relating the process to the engineers who developed the kneading propeller for the bread-making machine. The externalized knowledge was then combined with the engineers' existing knowledge. By internalizing this combination between externalized knowledge and their own understandings, the engineers were able to embed the externalized knowledge into the design of the home bakery machine.

In a later article, Nonaka and Konno (1998) introduce the idea of *ba* – derived from the work of the Japanese philosopher Kitaro Nishida – as the place or platform for advancing individual and/or collective knowledge. *Ba* is presented as a central feature of the four elements in the SECI knowledge conversion process. According to the two researchers, knowledge resides in *ba*, which is a shared space for emerging relationships. When separated from *ba*, knowledge becomes information. By participating in *ba*, an individual can transcend their own limited perspective and, through the synthesis of rationality and intuition, engage in creativity at each stage of the SECI model.

Although the SECI model is widely cited in knowledge management literature, it has also been the subject of criticism. For instance, Stephen Gourlay (2006) argues that the basis of empirical evidence that supports the model is unconvincing and that the assumption that tacit knowledge can be converted into explicit knowledge is open to question (as discussed here in Chapter 3). Although Nonaka and Takeuchi draw on Polanyi's distinction between tacit and explicit knowledge, they overlook Polanyi's view that all knowledge must be tacitly understood. Others still have highlighted that a model developed in a Japanese management context lacks universal relevance (Glisby and Holden, 2003). Despite this criticism, the SECI model does provide a useful means of thinking about how knowledge is generated within companies through the interactions of individuals. In the next section we turn to contexts within and beyond the boundaries of the firm, to explore how knowledge may be shared and generated in communities.

Knowledge communities, creativity, and innovation

Knowledge communities of one sort or another have always been important facilitators of creativity and innovation. In the late eighteenth century, for instance, the Lunar Society of Birmingham, in the United Kingdom, was an informal learned society that regularly brought together prominent figures of the Enlightenment such as James Watt, Erasmus Darwin, Josiah Wedgwood, and Joseph Priestley. The Lunar Society was also associated with a more widely distributed group, whose members corresponded by mail. In this way new ideas were developed and critiqued by a range of leading eighteenth-century thinkers. With the power of the Internet and the complex tools for long-distance communication, it is currently possible to sustain extensive knowledge communities capable of facilitating significant advances in knowledge. For instance, in today's world, scientists such as those described by Karin Knorr-Cetina (1999) in her book *Epistemic Cultures* engage in global networks through interaction online, attendance at international conferences, secondments and exchanges between public and private laboratories, collaborative international research projects, and so on. Such knowledge communities form what Knorr-Cetina calls epistemic cultures, whose purpose is the advancement of knowledge in a particular field. Such communities are not confined to science but exist in every field of knowledge. With the Internet and with relatively cheap international travel, these communities facilitate the global circulation of knowledge, which in turn accelerates the creation of new knowledge.

Communities facilitate the retention and transfer of knowledge; but they also have knowledge-creating capacities. Indeed, since the early 1990s, communities have received much attention from scholars and management practitioners as facilitators and sites of learning and knowledge generation (Amin and Roberts, 2008). This interest in community at an organizational level has been paralleled by a growing recognition of the importance of community to the operation of economic activity more generally (Bowles and Gintis, 2002). Community, through the provision of social infrastructure and social capital – which includes trust and reputation – underpins commercial business activity. Moreover, social interaction is a powerful source of creative stimulus; free from the imperatives of ownership and control, ideas can flow freely among community participants. In a bid to secure competitiveness, companies large and small are seeking to harness the innovative resources emerging in social environments and through local and distributed communities of all sorts.

Of the literature on community and knowledge production, it is the branch dealing with communities of practice that has gained significant influence in the field of knowledge management. The notion of communities of practice was originally developed by Jean Lave and Etienne Wenger (1991) in their seminal study of situated learning in the context of five apprenticeships – namely those of Yucatec midwives, Vai and Gola tailors, naval quartermasters, meat cutters, and non-drinking alcoholics. The two researchers define a community of practice as 'a set of relations among persons, activity, and world, over time and in relation with other tangential and overlapping communities of practice'. (Lave and Wenger, 1991: 98). Relationships and social interaction are central to knowledge and learning in communities that coalesce around specific practices. By participating in a community of practice, initially as a legitimate peripheral participant, members gain access, through learning in practice, to the community's knowledge resources. In addition, newcomers to a community who bring their knowledge and experiences from other contexts may influence the development of knowledge within the community by engaging in the negotiation of meaning.

Through a study of insurance claims processors, Wenger (1998) went on to develop a detailed understanding of the social dynamics of communities of practice, arguing that they are important places of negotiation, learning, meaning, and identity. According to him, members of communities of practice interact with one another, establishing norms and relationships through *mutual engagement*; they are bound together by a sense of *joint enterprise*; and over time they produce a *shared repertoire* of communal resources such as language, routines, artefacts, and stories (Wenger, 1998: 72–84). By working together, members of a community of practice learn from one another and solve problems collectively; in so doing, they share existing knowledge and generate new knowledge.

For Wenger, communities of practice may be part of a number of constellations of communities of practice, which share a variety of characteristics and are sustained by interactions among practices involving boundary processes. Boundary processes through which knowledge can be shared include brokering, the joint use of boundary objects, boundary interactions, and cross-disciplinary projects. These processes often occur simultaneously and support one another. Through them, ideas can travel across boundaries and can be reinterpreted and adapted in the process of being adopted within various practices. As styles and discourses spread across an entire constellation, their absorption into specific practices generates new knowledge, because they may be integrated into these various practices in very different ways. In the context of the insurance claims processors' unit studied by Wenger, that unit's community of practice was part of an organization made up of several such communities. The supervisor of the unit participated simultaneously in a number of communities of practice – both her own claims' processing unit and the local management unit. In this way she acted as a boundary-spanner, sharing knowledge across the constellation of practice that existed within the company. It is often around the boundaries of communities that the conflicting perspectives held by boundary-spanners lead to the development of new knowledge. The clashes arising from difference can create the spark for new knowledge. Bringing together different and sometimes conflicting perspectives can stimulate a process of forging novel approaches.

In a later volume targeted at management practitioners, Wenger, together with his co-authors McDermott and Snyder (2002), extended the notion of communities of practice to distributed groups within large organizations such as Shell Oil Company, McKinsey & Company, and the World Bank. Although communities originate in a local context, sustained and repeated interaction across distance may create new spatially extensive communities and constellations.

Since Lave and Wenger's original elaboration of the concept of community of practice as a site of learning and knowledge creation embedded and situated in social practices, with members engaging in face-to-face interaction, this idea has been extended and developed in many different contexts. Knowledge management practitioners and human resource managers have taken up the communities of practice approach as a way of managing knowledge workers in a variety of organizational environments. The idea has, nevertheless, been subject to criticism, and its limits highlighted (Roberts, 2006). For instance, the use of the term 'community' has been recognized as problematic. This is in part because of the positive connotations that this term carries, which neglect power dimensions and the potential rigidities inherent in such social structures. Furthermore, the appropriateness of the term 'community' for the wide array of groupings to which it is applied has been questioned. Lindkvist (2005), for example, proposes the idea of 'collectivities of practice' for short-term projects, and Brown and Duguid (2001) prefer the term 'networks of practice' for all but the smallest co-located organizational groupings.

Even so, the notion of communities of practice has been extended to include distantiated social interactions (that is, social interactions across distance), such as those that occur within online communities. Technological developments – including the Internet and the rise of Web 2.0 with its vast array of socially interactive platforms – have facilitated the development of online and virtual communities that stimulate rich multimedia engagement. Accordingly, it is necessary to recognize the variety that exists among conceptualizations of communities of practice. To capture this variety, in collaboration with my colleague Ash Amin, I developed the typology presented in Table 5.1 (Amin and Roberts, 2008). Here communities of practice are differentiated in terms of varieties of knowing in action. Four types of knowing associated with four distinct yet often overlapping activities are captured in this typology. The development of knowledge in communities that form around these four types of knowing requires distinctive patterns of social interaction and spatial characteristics, which give rise to different sorts of innovation and organizational dynamics. In relation to innovation, for instance, craft- and task-based communities focus on the reproduction

Table 5.1 Varieties of knowing in action

Activity	Type of knowledge	Social interaction			Innovation	Organizational dynamic
		Proximity/nature of communication	Temporal aspects	Nature of social ties		
Craft/task based	• Aesthetic, kinaesthetic, and embodied knowledge.	Knowledge transfer requires co-location and face-to-face communication; importance of demonstration.	Long-lived and apprenticeship-based; developing sociocultural institutional structures.	Interpersonal trust – mutuality through the performance of shared tasks.	Customized, incremental.	Hierarchically managed; open to new members.
Professional	• Specialized expert knowledge acquired through prolonged periods of education and training. • Declarative knowledge. • Mind–matter and technologically embodied (aesthetic and kinaesthetic dimensions).	Co-location required in the development of professional status for communication through demonstration; not as important thereafter.	Long-lived and slow to change; developing formal regulatory institutions.	Institutional trust based on professional standards of conduct.	Incremental or radical but strongly bound by institutional/ professional rules; radical innovation stimulated by contact with other communities.	Large hierarchically managed organizations or small peer-managed organizations; institutional restrictions on the entry of new members.

Activity	Type of knowledge	Social interaction					Organizational dynamic
		Proximity/nature of communication	Temporal aspects	Nature of social ties	Innovation		
Epistemic/ creative	• Specialized and expert knowledge, including standards and codes (including meta-codes). • Exist to extend knowledge base. • Temporary creative coalitions (by virtue of knowledge changing rapidly).	Spatial and/or relational proximity; communication facilitated through a combination of face-to-face and distantiated contact.	Short-lived, drawing on institutional resources from a variety of epistemic/ creative fields.	Trust based on reputation and expertise; weak social ties.	High-energy, radical innovation	Group/project managed; open to those with a reputation in the field; management through intermediaries and boundary objects.
Virtual	• Codified and tacit from codified. • Exploratory and exploitative.	Social interaction mediated through technology – face-to-screen; distantiated communication; rich web-based anthropology.	Long- and short-lived; developing through fast and asynchronous interaction.	Weak social ties; reputational trust; object orientation.	Incremental and radical	Carefully managed by community moderators or technological sequences; open, but self-regulating.

Source: Amin and Roberts (2008: 357).

of skills and therefore produce incremental innovation, often by customizing products, while professional communities that reproduce specialist knowledge engage in incremental and radical innovation. Epistemic communities are focused on the advancement of specialist knowledge, and therefore they engage in radical innovation. Finally, virtual communities, which involve a wide range of activities through technologically mediated interaction across distance, can engage in either incremental or radical innovation.

Furthermore, in professional, epistemic, and virtual communities, relational proximity – achieved through distantiated communication and occasional face-to-face engagement – can facilitate high levels of rich interaction across distance, thereby allowing those communities to become virtual places for innovative activity that is dislocated from territorial space. Indeed, by linking spatially distributed innovative capacities, communities of practice offer opportunities for the development of new knowledge.

Although communities may be seen as a 'supplement' to formal organizations, they are not the same as them, no matter whether they are situated within, between, or beyond their boundaries. Boundary-crossing communities give organizations opportunities to access knowledge from the wider environment. Such communities include the social and professional ones in which an organization's employees participate. By maintaining links to external communities, organizations maintain channels through which external knowledge can be accessed. Interaction with such communities adds to the porosity of the organization's boundaries and thereby to its flexibility and ability to respond to changing market opportunities and challenges.

Conclusion

As this chapter has shown, knowledge management can support creative and innovative activity, particularly when it is focused on the exploitation of existing knowledge in new ways. Knowledge management can provide easy access to existing knowledge or can assist in the collation and analysis of the information required for major breakthroughs or highly creative and radical innovations. However, it is important to recognize that knowledge management can also stifle the exploration for new knowledge. First, there is a danger that knowledge may become path-dependent through the codification of knowledge. Second, when new knowledge challenges existing organizational practices, those with vested interests in maintaining the status quo are likely to resist change. Third, where organizations are characterized by strong communities, the norms and values of such communities can create significant barriers to change. In a fast-changing business context, the development of rigid knowledge management practices can be counter-productive for firms that depend on creativity for their success. This is not to say that creativity cannot benefit from structures that support the acquisition, retention, and transfer of knowledge, but rather that such structures must serve the creative process rather than control or suppress it.

In discussions of knowledge in relation to creativity and innovation, there is little recognition of issues concerning the lack of knowledge or the unknown. Sometimes creativity requires a leap into the unknown. Yet knowledge management, with its focus on existing knowledge, can overlook this aspect of creativity. In the next chapter we explore the unknown through the concepts of ignorance, forgetting, and unlearning and we consider their relation to knowledge management.

▰▰▰▰ Notes

1. For further details, see http://crash.curtin.edu.au/ (accessed 2 February 2014).
2. Visit CERN's website at http://home.web.cern.ch/ (accessed 11 March 2014).

6

Ignorance, Forgetting, and Unlearning

And he [Socrates] used to say that he knew nothing except that very thing – that he knew nothing.

Diogenes Laertius 2.32

As the preceding chapters have shown, knowledge management is concerned with creating, acquiring, capturing, sharing, and using knowledge in organizations in order to improve performance. Knowledge management practices can be employed when knowledge is easily identified and valued. But what happens when knowledge is absent, or difficult to identify or appreciate? What happens when ignorance takes the place of knowledge? Knowledge management approaches tend to ignore such circumstances, or at best they include them as uncertainties or risks. Ignorance is a topic that is rarely given more than a cursory consideration in the mainstream management literature. Moreover, when ignorance is considered, it is often viewed as something to be removed through learning and the production of more knowledge or, when it relates to consumers or competitors, as something to be maintained and exploited through restricted access to knowledge. This chapter is devoted to understanding ignorance and its relation to knowledge management. In addition, it is necessary to consider forgetting and unlearning as ways of regaining ignorance. I hear readers ask: surely, ignorance is the opposite of what is required to manage an organization effectively?

Certainly valuing ignorance is counterintuitive. Yet it is attracting increasing attention from scholars and practitioners in a number of fields, including sustainability and ecology (Vitek and Jackson, 2008; Gross, 2010). In the organizational context, managing the unknown need not concentrate merely on the control and minimization of ignorance; it can also deal with its productive employment – for instance, in creativity and innovation. Furthermore, as Nassim Nicholas Taleb (2007) suggests in his popular book *The Black Swan*, we need to be aware of our lack of knowledge if we are to improve our ability to cope with the unexpected. The potential value that managing ignorance might offer motivated my recent research on organizational ignorance (Roberts, 2013). Drawing on this work, I will show in this chapter how an understanding of ignorance can be of value to managers, and especially to those engaged in the management of knowledge. It is necessary to begin by defining ignorance and its relation to knowledge. Following this, I will give an account of how an understanding of ignorance can be of value to the management of knowledge. The chapter will end by considering efforts to regain ignorance through forgetting and unlearning.

What is ignorance and how does it relate to knowledge?

In today's knowledge-based economy, it is a popular misconception that, as knowledge expands, ignorance diminishes. A dynamic relationship does exist between the two. Yet, as the philosopher Karl Popper notes:

> The more we learn about the world, the deeper our learning, the more conscious, specific, and articulate will be our knowledge of what we do not know, our knowledge of our ignorance. For this, indeed, is the main source of our ignorance – the fact that our knowledge can only be finite, while our ignorance must necessarily be infinite. (2004: 38)

So, as our knowledge expands, so too does our knowledge of our ignorance. For example, as new knowledge leads to the production of new chemical compounds, we become aware of our ignorance of the outcomes of a potentially vast number of new chemical interactions.

Despite the growing amounts of knowledge and information at our disposal in the contemporary era of big data and despite the expanding availability of computing power, the ability of humans to process all existing information remains limited. The unprecedented scale of information collection facilitated by information and communications technologies (ICTs) gives rise to challenges, for example the need for classification. The more information is collected, the greater the management task. Indeed the management of information produces more information, because, as data are organized, more information is produced. For instance, when you use a supermarket loyalty card such as the Tesco Clubcard, the information about the items that you purchase delivers yet more information about your lifestyle. Next time you are waiting at the supermarket checkout, look at the items that the person in front of you is purchasing: it is pretty easy to assess from the information gained from such items whether someone is health-conscious in their eating habits. The collection and classification of information produce many opportunities for recombinations that are designed to generate new information and knowledge; but they also add to the mounting difficulty of managing ever-greater quantities of information and knowledge. Information overload thus results in a kind of ignorance, because our capacity to manage and comprehend information is not keeping pace with its seemingly exponential growth. As individuals, we are subject to bounded rationality (Simon, 1955); we cannot know and understand everything, choices have to be made. Even at an organizational level, bounded rationality reveals itself in what Herbert Simon (1973) calls 'limited managerial attention'. Many important decisions, whether at the level of the individual, the organization, or society as a whole, have to be made in the absence of complete information or knowledge. More often than not, then, we act in ignorance. But what is ignorance?

Ignorance is typically defined as a lack of knowledge or information (*Oxford Dictionary of English*, 2003: 862). If knowledge is defined as justified true belief, ignorance can be viewed as the absence or the distortion of justified true belief. One might then argue that ignorance is the absence of empirically valid knowledge. However, as Michael Smithson (1989) notes in his *Ignorance and Uncertainty*, the adoption of this approach requires established criteria for absolute knowledge or truth; yet knowledge may be socially constructed, so both truth and its absence depend on a given perspective or system of belief. Hence ignorance, just like knowledge, may also be socially constructed.

Related to ignorance is the condition of being ignorant – that is, of lacking knowledge. To be ignorant is associated with being rude, discourteous, or stupid. A person with no knowledge may be referred to as an ignoramus. Moreover, 'to ignore' also designates a failure or a refusal to notice something or someone. Ignorance is then defined either in relation to an absence of knowledge, a failure to understand knowledge – ignorance about knowledge; or in relation to the refusal to recognize knowledge – ignorance from the suppression of knowledge.

Any attempt to gain an appreciation of ignorance is dependent on one's awareness of its existence. Ignorance as *known unknowns* denotes knowledge of what is known about the limits of knowledge; there are certain things that we know that we do not know. In contrast, ignorance as *unknown unknowns* refers to a total absence of knowledge, a state in which we are not aware of our ignorance. Unknown unknowns are completely beyond anticipation, and, as Matthias Gross (2010) notes, the revelation of such ignorance can be a source of surprise. Even so, experience tells us that some unknown unknowns will be revealed at some point in the future. Both known unknowns and unknown unknowns derive from the absence of knowledge.

In 2002 the then US Secretary of Defense, Donald H. Rumsfeld, elaborated on these two important types of ignorance when answering a question about reports that no evidence existed to link Baghdad with terrorist organizations (see Box 6.1). Interestingly, Rumsfeld's comments attracted ridicule in many media outlets, demonstrating a resistance on the part of reporters to take ignorance and its implications seriously. Yet Rumsfeld clearly outlined an important distinction between ignorance as known unknowns and ignorance as unknown unknowns and, in the process, he stimulated debate about ignorance in military affairs.

Box 6.1   Donald Rumsfeld on ignorance

QUESTION: In regard to Iraq weapons of mass destruction and terrorists, is there any evidence to indicate that Iraq has attempted to or is willing to supply terrorists with weapons of mass destruction? Because there are reports that there is no evidence of a direct link between Baghdad and some of these terrorist organizations.

RUMSFELD: Reports that say that something hasn't happened are always interesting to me, because as we know, there are known knowns; there are things we know we know. We also know there are known unknowns; that is to say we know there are some things we do not know. But there are also unknown unknowns – the ones we don't know we don't know. And if one looks throughout the history of our country and other free countries, it is the latter category that tend to be the difficult ones.

Source: Extract from DoD News Briefing: Secretary Rumsfeld and Gen. Myers, February 12, 2002, 11:30 AM EDT. Available at: www.defense. gov/Transcripts/Transcript.aspx?TranscriptID=2636 (accessed 13 February 2013).

Ignorance can also result from ignorance about knowledge, which gives rise to *knowable known unknowns, unknown knowns*, and *errors*. A *knowable known unknown* differs from a known unknown in that it is knowable once the motivation and resources necessary to acquire the knowledge are given. *Unknown knowns* are things we do not know that we know. They include the tacit knowledge that individuals are not always aware that they possess. Unknown knowns denote ignorance about existing knowledge rather than just unqualified ignorance. Such ignorance does not prevent the use of unknown knowledge. *Errors* arise from distortion, when they are founded on confusion or inaccuracy, or from incompleteness, when they are based on uncertainty or absence.

The possibility of errors lies in the limitations of human cognitive capacity. Hence, as the saying goes, to err is to be human.

Another type of ignorance emerges from the refusal to recognize knowledge or its unconscious suppression: this would include *taboos* and *denials*. A *taboo* is socially constructed ignorance in the form of a social prohibition or a ban on certain knowledge, perhaps because it is viewed as dangerous or polluting. For example, knowledge about sexual reproduction before marriage is taboo in some societies. *Denials* are acts of ignoring or repressing knowledge that is too painful to face or that does not fit with one's current understandings of the world. Knowledge that does not correspond with one's existing cognitive frameworks creates a degree of dissonance, which can challenge one's current understanding. Tolerating such cognitive dissonance through denial is a common response. Denials can also be described as wilful ignorance or wilful blindness and can exist at the level of the individual or the group.

Ignorance also arises from the conscious suppression of knowledge through *secrecy*, either by individuals or by organizations. Ignorance arises for individuals and organizations when they are subject to the secrecy of others. Certain types of secrets may be socially sanctioned, such as those arising from the individual's right to privacy. Thus, ignorance can also be identified with *privacy* – the ability of an individual or group of individuals to restrict access to, or information about, themselves. Unlike secrecy, privacy is multilateral in nature and is enshrined in the laws of many countries and in supranational declarations, including the United Nations' Universal Declaration of Human Rights. Social and cultural practices also determine patterns of privacy. Giving someone their own privacy may be seen as polite and may determine individuals to suppress their own curiosity about and knowledge of the lives of others. In this sense, privacy can create knowable known unknowns. Technologies, and the way they are employed in social interaction, are challenging the abilities of the state, businesses, and individuals to suppress knowledge through secrecy and privacy. For instance, in recent years the website Wikileaks has become renowned for its disclosure of state secrets, while speculation on the private lives of celebrities and public figures by members of social media sites like Twitter is challenging the enforcement of privacy laws. As knowledge becomes more difficult to suppress, the power derived from its control is increasingly questioned.

The sources of ignorance and its relation to knowledge, together with the types of ignorance associated with these sources, are summarized in Figure 6.1.

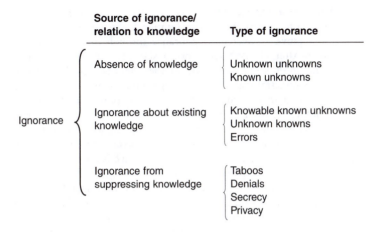

Figure 6.1 Types and sources of ignorance
Source: Compiled from Roberts (2013: 227–9).

Having considered the nature of ignorance and its relation to knowledge, we can now consider how understandings of ignorance can be valuable to organizations and, in particular, to the development of effective knowledge management practices.

What are the benefits of managing ignorance?

Even though ignorance is an intrinsic element in social organizations, it has attracted limited interest from management scholars. Moreover, these scholars' reflections on organizational ignorance merely focus on how to eliminate it through better knowledge management practices. Michael Zack's (1999) contribution is typical of this approach. Zack classifies organizational ignorance in relation to four knowledge-processing problems: uncertainty – not having enough information; complexity – having to process more information than one can manage or understand; ambiguity – not having a conceptual framework for interpreting the information; and equivocality – having several competing or contradictory conceptual frameworks. For Zack, each of these knowledge-processing problems can be alleviated through the development of the correct knowledge management infrastructure.

Clearly the negative connotations that accompany the concept of ignorance go some way towards accounting for its neglect and for the desire to remove or overcome ignorance through the application of knowledge. After all, isn't ignorance a sign of managerial incompetence? The sheer scope and scale of the methodological challenges involved in undertaking research on ignorance may account for its neglect in the management literature. While ignorance in the form of known unknowns or knowable known unknowns can be explored, ignorance as unknown unknowns is very difficult to identify. Indeed, unknown unknowns can only be envisaged through speculation, or in retrospect. Besides, the extent to which ignorance is absolute – that is, a common, universally given set of beliefs – or relative – in other words unevenly distributed between individuals, organizations, and social and cultural groups across time and space – will also inform the degree to which organizational ignorance can be investigated.

Given all these obstacles, ignorance is ignored. When aspects of the unknown are considered, these are more often than not aspects acceptable in management discourse, such as uncertainty, or complexity. Yet, as March and Simon note, 'organizations are systems of coordinated action among individuals and groups whose preferences, information, interests, or knowledge differ' (1993: 2). These differences in knowledge, then, also imply a difference in patterns of ignorance between individuals within organizations.

Given the existence of so many and so often unacknowledged unknowns, it is necessary to incorporate into management activity – particularly knowledge management activity – their potential impact. Indeed, recognizing the limits of knowledge and acknowledging ignorance is, in the Socratic tradition, a form of wisdom. So, if we think about ignorance in terms of the data–information–knowledge–wisdom hierarchy discussed in Chapter 1 (see Figure 1.2), ignorance as a form of wisdom can be placed at the top of this hierarchy. This is because an understanding of the unknown brings with it openness to the unexpected and an appreciation of the fact that change presents opportunities as well as threats. Given the rapidly evolving technological, sociocultural, and political context of the contemporary world, readiness for the unexpected is an important source of competitiveness, as it allows for a fast and effective response to changing conditions. For instance, the Internet, with its ability to facilitate the fast growth of ecommerce, introduced many unknowns in the late 1990s. Those retailers that recognized their own ignorance, yet grasped the opportunities offered by online retailing, are in much stronger competitive positions today than those that have only recently begun to engage in ecommerce. Indeed late entry into online retailing (or not entering at all) has been fatal to some retailers – for instance, to the British electrical retailer Comet, which entered administration in 2012 after almost 80 years of trading.

Organizational ignorance takes a number of forms. First, it can be defined as the all-pervasive ignorance of the organization's members, or as the relative ignorance between members across different parts of the organization. Second, organizational ignorance is relative to that of other organizations and external parties: competitors, suppliers, customers. Third, organizational ignorance can arise from earlier organizational decisions, such as investment in the development of knowledge in one area at the expense of another. Finally (and perhaps surprisingly), organizational ignorance can include unknowns unique to individuals in the organization when it is actively sought and deployed by the organization; this point will be illustrated shortly.

Organizational unknown unknowns and known unknowns

In an organizational context, an *unknown unknown* is a state of ignorance at a specific point in time for all members of the organization. The existence of unknown unknowns in an abstract sense has been recognized for some time in organizations concerned with high-risk research and development (R&D) – like those in the field of aerospace engineering, where the phrase has long been abbreviated to 'unk unks' (Longstaff, 2005). An organization may discover the existence of prior unknown unknowns – for instance, through the recruitment of staff with knowledge sets that are new to the organization, the acquisition of new equipment, R&D, the purchase of consultancy services, interaction with customers and suppliers, and the actions of competitors. Indeed external actors, like competing organizations, may actively construct unknown unknowns for their rivals by disseminating false information about their intentions or by restricting the circulation of newly acquired knowledge. Therefore the knowledge management practices of organizations concerned with the protection of knowledge actively perpetuate ignorance among competitors. Recognizing that the organization is exposed to unknown unknowns can stimulate the kind of speculative thinking that has the aim of transforming these unknown unknowns into known unknowns. Techniques that can be used to uncover such ignorance include scenario planning – also known as scenario thinking or scenario analysis – which involves combining the known and the unknown to produce a number of internally consistent scenarios of the future that incorporate a wide range of possibilities (Schoemaker, 1995; Wright and Cairns, 2011). Foresight studies, by anticipating the future, also seek to uncover existing unknowns (Loveridge, 2009). Since knowledge management is concerned with acquiring new knowledge, such techniques could be usefully deployed as a component of a knowledge management strategy.

Organizational *known unknowns* indicate an awareness that certain knowledge is beyond that possessed by the organization and its members. Although they may be overcome through learning, the recruitment of staff, R&D, the purchase of knowledge embedded in capital equipment, or the purchase of consultancy services, known unknowns may – like unknown unknowns – extend beyond the organization. As a result, there is no guarantee that investment in extending the organization's knowledge will remove this form of ignorance. Known unknowns give organizations choices in terms of where to focus their strategic resources. For instance, an organization may withdraw from areas that expose it to known unknowns by refocusing its activities or by outsourcing exposure to such ignorance. In a sense, outsourcing certain activities indicates a recognition of the limits of knowledge and of its management within organizations. Indeed, organizations regularly outsource exposure to ignorance about various potentially damaging events through the purchase of insurances.

Known unknowns drive creativity and innovation in all parts of the organization, from R&D and design to customer relations, marketing, and human resource management. In a sense, ignorance is necessary for learning and discovery to take place. However, if this ignorance is neglected, then so too are the opportunities for learning. Hence, although knowledge management practices focus on acquiring knowledge through learning, it is important to tolerate and, where possible, identify areas of ignorance in order to stimulate a climate of curiosity and creativity. It is not only the case that ignorance may stimulate the search for new knowledge; surprisingly, the lack of knowledge – unknown unknowns – can also be an important element in facilitating the creativity of groups within the organization. This is because the naivety and innocence of the young or those inexperienced in a particular field of expertise can be important forces driving forward the boundaries of knowledge. The development of new ideas and products often requires the creators to think 'outside the box'. Hence ignorance of the box – in terms of existing knowledge in a particular field – can facilitate creativity.

The work of the film director Orson Welles provides a useful illustration of how the ignorance of an individual, if appropriately deployed, can result in the development of new knowledge. His first film, *Citizen Kane* (1941), is widely recognized as one of the world's most famous and highly rated films. Yet Welles produced this film at the age of 25, with no previous film-making experience. Almost 20 years later, Welles explained where he got the confidence to make the film:

> Ignorance, ignorance, sheer ignorance – you know there's no confidence to equal it. It's only when you know something about a profession, I think, that you're timid or careful. ... I thought you could do anything with a camera, you know, that the eye could do and the imagination could do and if you come up from the bottom in the film business you're taught all the things that the cameraman doesn't want to attempt for fear he will be criticized for having failed. And in this case I had a cameraman who didn't care if he was criticized if he failed, and I didn't know there were things you couldn't do, so anything I could think up in my dreams I attempted to photograph. (Wheldon, 2002: 80–1)

Welles' ignorance of film-making techniques allowed him to challenge the boundaries of existing knowledge in the profession and to develop innovative practices, including novel cinematographic practices and narrative structures that continue to influence film-making today. Nevertheless, it is important to note that Welles achieved this through the combination of his own ignorance and the knowledge and experience of other members of the film's production team. By the same token, organizations may employ the ignorance of an ignoramus to identify new possibilities and use that ignorant member as a catalyst for creativity.

Newcomers to an organization are normally ignorant of many of its norms and practices. Although they may join an organization because of their specialist knowledge, they are also valuable because, by combining this knowledge with their ignorance of the organization, they are able to ask questions that would never occur to existing members. In this way, the ignorance of new members can help existing members to adopt a new perspective, and this has potentially beneficial consequences for new-knowledge creation. The systematic management of knowledge can generate barriers to creativity. Organizational structures and systems, even when they take the form of communities, can stand in the way of change when this process (or its result) is not aligned with current norms and practices. New members can help to challenge this kind of resistance. The type of creative capacity that can arise from the adoption of the ignorance of newcomers can also be achieved through what March (1976: 81) calls 'the technology of foolishness', which is realized through playfulness and the rejection of accepted knowledge and practices in favour of the irrational and the unknown. Only by recognizing the potential of ignorance to stimulate creativity does it become possible to identify methods to harness this very potential. Of course, ignorance alone is unlikely to be productive; it must be combined with existing organizational knowledge if it is to facilitate constructive outcomes. Hence an important objective of a knowledge management strategy should be to make knowledge resources easily available to support the development of new knowledge through the creativity that arises from ignorance.

Organizational knowable known unknowns, unknown knowns, and errors

An organizational *knowable known unknown* is a form of ignorance that the organization is not motivated to overcome through the expenditure of the necessary resources. The choice regarding the acquisition of knowledge about knowable known unknowns will depend on the costs and benefits involved and on the organization's strategy. Where a knowable known unknown becomes of significance to the organization's activities, an investment will be made in the acquisition of the appropriate knowledge – be that through learning, staff recruitment, R&D or the purchase of knowledge embedded in capital equipment or consultancy services. Such ignorance reflects the knowledge priorities of organizations. So, even though knowledge is the most significant organizational resource (Grant, 1996), choices have to be made about what knowledge to prioritize and what areas of ignorance to tolerate. Within organizations, knowledge and ignorance will be unevenly distributed. Consequently, knowable known unknowns can be sustained within, or confined to, parts of the organization through a process of specialization and coordination. In this way the organization is able to economize on cognitive resources, which in turn allows for an uneven internal distribution of knowledge across the organization and within groups.

Organizational *unknown knowns* represent knowledge that is unrecognized in the organization. Such knowledge may be embedded in tacit routines, in collective practices, or in both. The workforce or the management does not always acknowledge unknown knowns and they are not easily reflected in the organization's formal structure. Thus an organization can have knowledge it is unaware of, and therefore unable to manage. Of course, knowledge management practices have evolved from their original focus on information and the codification of knowledge towards a broader understanding, which recognizes the significance of tacit knowledge. The rise in popularity of communities of practice as a means of managing the tacit knowledge embedded in social contexts is an indication of this trend. However, while the existence and significance of tacit knowledge are recognized, its specific qualities are not always easy to identify – and we need to be aware of this limitation.

The existence of unknown knowns may be demonstrated in retrospect. For instance, knowledge of what a company's archive contains may be lost when those responsible for maintaining it retire. But, when a particular piece of knowledge is sought, it may become apparent, through archival research, that this knowledge was once available to the organization. Knowledge of the skills embedded in the workforce may be forgotten due to poor human resource management systems, and this would result in efforts to reintroduce skills that already exist. In some cases, then, this kind of ignorance can be attributed to poor knowledge management practices.

On the other hand, ignorance in the form of unknown knowns may also underpin creativity. Under the description of 'intuition', unarticulated knowledge has been recognized for some time as an important element in the act of creation (Koestler, 1976). Thus acknowledging and valuing unknown knowing in the form of instincts, intuition, and insights unsubstantiated by evidence has a role in the general management of ignorance. Of course, these types of unknown knowns are difficult to incorporate into knowledge management practices; but just recognizing that they exist is an important step towards integrating them into a comprehensive knowledge management approach.

Organizational *error* is ignorance arising from the bounded rationality of individual organizational actors and the limitations of managerial attention. Hence a limited cognitive capacity (which is in the nature of human cognition) creates scope for organizational error. Rapidly and perpetually changing environments stretch the organization's cognitive resources, thereby increasing the capacity for organizational error. Organizational error can often be traced to the actions of individual organizational actors or to a failure in organizational systems. For example, Kruger and Dunning (1999) provide evidence that individuals have difficulties assessing their own level of competence; their inflated self-assessments can lead to error. Although organization-wide systems such as expert computer-based systems can be introduced to minimize individual error, managers themselves, and those who design the systems, may also have inflated views about their own competence – with implications for the organization as a whole and for the systems upon which it depends. As knowledge advances, our understanding of problems becomes more complex and our efforts to control error become more sophisticated.

Although error can result in a major catastrophe, it is often in times of crisis that major advances in knowledge are made. As the saying goes, necessity is the mother of invention. Consequently, errors can lead to learning and to the development of new knowledge over time.

An example is the Deepwater Horizon oil spill in the Gulf of Mexico in 2010, which resulted in one of the USA's worst environmental disasters (Sherwell, 2010). During almost three months of battle to stem the flow of oil, major untried engineering feats were undertaken, in an intensive period of creative activity simulated by the urgent need to find a workable solution (BBC, 2010).

Organizational taboos, denials, secrecy, and privacy

Ignorance is unambiguously socially constructed when its source is the suppression of knowledge. Organizational *taboos* represent ignorance embedded in the social and cultural context inside and/or outside the organization. Taboos may be actively cultivated in an organization in order to influence the behaviour of its members. The induction of new organizational members may involve the promotion of certain areas of knowledge, particular behaviours, and working patterns to the exclusion of others. For instance, the behaviours, practices, and methods of work in a top international accountancy firm like Ernst & Young, which belongs to a highly regulated field of professional practice, will be very different from those at the Internet giant Google, which seeks to challenge existing online services through continual innovation. While particular ways of working are promoted, others are neglected and may even be regarded as inappropriate or taboo. For example, playing computer games at work may be fine at Google, but this would be taboo in an accountancy organization where every 15 minutes of an employee's time is billable.

Taboos may also derive from the external environment. Organizations may learn to exploit taboos by using them to promote certain products or services to customers or by using them in management strategies. However, at the same time, by supporting certain attitudes, taboos can act as a barrier to the introduction of new knowledge, thereby potentially reducing the competitiveness of organizations that operate in fast-changing environments. An effective knowledge management strategy needs to take into account how taboos can lead to the suppression of certain knowledge within organizations, and it should be prepared to challenge taboos when they risk the competitiveness of the organization.

Organizational *denials* occur when the values and norms embedded in the organization blind its members to knowledge that does not fit easily with the existing frameworks of understanding. Organizational denials can also result from what Irving Janis (1972) calls 'groupthink'. In the search for unanimity, organizational members ignore evidence that contradicts the validity of a group's decision. Evidence of such denials can be found in the organizational debacles of Enron and

Lehman Brothers. In both cases, employees articulated concerns about the functioning of the business, yet the management of these organizations failed to take the warnings on board, and both organizations eventually filed for bankruptcy. Denial can, then, prevent the implementation of new approaches to management in a timely fashion.

In addition, organizational denial can prevent creative and positive responses to rapid environmental change, as witnessed in the film and music industry, where digital technologies and the Internet are facilitating widespread piracy and thus making some traditional business models obsolete. Even so, the large entertainment conglomerates cling to the previous business model (Knopper, 2009). By contrast, Apple Inc., a relatively recent entrant to the entertainment distribution market, seized the opportunities offered by the Internet and transformed the sector through the introduction of new technologies for the purchase and consumption of music in the form of iTunes and iPods. In the process, Apple Inc. has secured significant market power.

Organizational *secrecy* also holds relevance for the understanding of organizational ignorance. Secrets within organizations create deliberate areas of ignorance, which has consequences for the distribution of organizational power. Organizations may encourage the suppression of knowledge where its release might have a negative impact on performance. For instance, group cohesion may be threatened if knowledge of differentials between individual members' remuneration becomes public. It is therefore common in private organizations for information about individuals' salaries to be held in confidence. Moreover, despite growing interest and participation in open innovation (Chesbrough, 2006), secrecy pervades creativity in the commercial sector. For example, trade secrets represent a strategic employment of ignorance through the suppression of knowledge (Proctor, 2008). Some trade secrets, like the recipe for Coca-Cola, become known in the sense that there is knowledge that the secret exists, but the knowledge content of the 'secret' remains suppressed. As noted in Chapter 4, the management of an organization's knowledge through intellectual property rights (IPRs) and through secrecy is an important means of protecting knowledge, and therefore an important element of any knowledge management strategy. Such strategies purposely sustain ignorance among competitors, consumers, and employees. As we have already seen, Apple Inc. is renowned for the level of secrecy that accompanies the development of new products: not only are competitors and consumers kept in the dark, but the employees who design components for new products do not know what the final product will be.

Organizational *privacy* refers to preserving a state of ignorance (or keeping people ignorant) about one's employees or customers; it reflects the organization's commitment to maintaining the privacy of individuals while it acquires the knowledge it needs in order to undertake its activities. Individual members may have to disclose certain knowledge to an organization – for example, concerning disability. Such information may be provided on the condition that it will be kept private and not widely circulated. The privacy of customers is often important as well; in areas like medicine and law, providers are bound by professional codes of conduct that ensure confidentiality about their customers. In such areas, the management of knowledge must be sensitive to the level of confidentiality required. While keeping records in computer files and transferring them by e-mail may be convenient, it is necessary to recognize the risk to privacy inherent in the electronic storage and transmission of information. We hear regular news stories about cyber-criminals stealing from companies information that often contains the names, addresses, and credit card details of customers. A contemporary debate in the United Kingdom concerns the centralization of the population's personal health records. There are great benefits to be derived for patients and medical research from the centralization of health records; but there is also a lack of trust in the ability of a centralized system to hold these data securely and to ensure that personal data are used anonymously and only for research purposes. Knowledge management systems and practices need to be sufficiently robust to maintain the right level of ignorance for the preservation of privacy. Moreover, they also need to inspire trust among their various stakeholders.

The recognition and protection of privacy supports the development of a relationship of trust between the organization and its members, customers, and suppliers. Furthermore, placing trust in an organization's members by allowing them high levels of autonomy and privacy in their working practices can be an important condition for the construction of a satisfactory work environment. The elimination of privacy in the workplace through the introduction of mechanisms of surveillance can severely impair trust and undermine working relations, leading to the loss of productive staff. Thus too much knowledge obtained by management through surveillance can have negative consequences for productivity. This is supported by the study of Alge et al. (2006), which identified links between information privacy and empowerment on the one hand and between empowerment and creative performance or organizational citizenship behaviour on the other. There are cases in which the management's ignorance about the activities of workers can have a positive impact on productivity. Moreover, from a managerial perspective, the maintenance of a degree of ignorance creates a position of vulnerability, which is a prerequisite for the development of a relationship of trust with employees, suppliers, and customers. All this shows that it is necessary to maintain the right balance between an active management of knowledge – achieved by monitoring, measuring, collecting, and analysing information – and giving individuals and groups autonomy over how they manage knowledge resources within the organization.

Clearly organizational ignorance is not as simple and straightforward as the absence of knowledge. While it is very much related to organizational knowledge, organizational ignorance is also independent from it in that it can be employed strategically – both within the organization and in the wider environment, in relation to customers, suppliers, and competitors. Importantly, ignorance is often not absolute, but relative to organizations and organizational actors. Accordingly, it can be mobilized at will and made to work for the benefit of individuals, groups, and organizations.

Regaining ignorance through forgetting and unlearning

Although knowledge and ignorance are intimately related, it would be wrong to think that ignorance is merely the absence of knowledge. Moreover, understandings of ignorance are not static. Gross (2010) argues that types of knowledge about the unknown interact over time in a recursive manner, with the result that unknowns may be transformed into new knowledge and, in the process, new limits of knowledge identified. Furthermore, it is important to recognize that knowledge may be forgotten and lost over time, with ignorance emerging where knowledge once existed. Time is an important dimension when we consider ignorance. Historical patterns of knowledge creation, learning, unlearning, and forgetting are all determinants of knowledge and ignorance at any specific point in time. There are also spatial dimensions to consider, for what is known in one place is not necessarily known in another. Ignorance, like knowledge, is not evenly distributed between individuals, groups, or organizations over time or space.

In the field of management there is increasing recognition of the importance of ignorance in the form of the removal of existing knowledge through unlearning and forgetting. Unlearning and forgetting allow for ignorance to be regained; thus they provide scope for new forms of understanding, unencumbered by orthodox perspectives. Top management is often replaced in a crisis because the dominance of its knowledge prevents the adoption of new practices. It is for this reason that Paul C. Nystrom and William H. Starbuck (1984) advocate continual unlearning as a means for managers to avoid crises.

Just as individuals forget, so too do organizations. If people stay with an organization long enough, they can get a feeling of déjà vu, as the same practices are introduced only a few years after they were abandoned.

Linda Argote (2013) has explored organizational forgetting in terms of knowledge depreciation in sectors such as shipbuilding, automobile manufacturing, and service franchising. In these sectors, organizations lose knowledge over time, for instance through the loss of staff from retirements, layoffs, or downsizing or through changes to production routines. Argote argues that organizations need to take account of this process of organizational forgetting if they are to avoid reductions in performance.

In the study of an international strategic alliance involving a major Cuban hotel chain and its international partners, Martin de Holan and Phillips (2004) found organizational forgetting to be an important part of the knowledge transfer process. They identify four types of organizational forgetting, two of which are accidental, namely the inability to retain new knowledge (dissipation) and the deterioration of knowledge (degradation). The other two can be considered purposeful: abandoning innovations (suspension) and managed unlearning (purging). All four types give rise to ignorance in the sense that knowledge is lost. Managers need to work to avoid the accidental forgetting, whereas purposeful forgetting requires encouragement. Purposeful organizational forgetting relates to efforts to regain ignorance. In Martin de Holan and Phillips' study, this occurred in the form of abandoned innovations, when new knowledge acquired through learning did not have value when applied to specific circumstances. For instance, when new organizational structures and operating procedures were introduced into a Cuban hotel, if they did not work they had to be quickly abandoned and the old structures and operating procedures were re-established. Managed unlearning occurs when the existing knowledge becomes a barrier to the introduction of new knowledge or to regaining old knowledge in cases where newly introduced knowledge proves to be inappropriate. Therefore unlearning can be an important prerequisite for the acquisition of new knowledge through learning.

Like organizational forgetting, unlearning remains woefully under-researched. Nevertheless, the need to engage in unlearning in order to make way for new learning has been recognized for some time. For instance, Bo Hedberg argued over 30 years ago that 'understanding involves both learning new knowledge and discarding obsolete and misleading knowledge. The discarding activity – unlearning – is as important a part of understanding as is adding new knowledge' (1981: 3). More recently, Eric W. K. Tsang (2008) examined organizational unlearning in relation to knowledge transfer in Sino-foreign joint ventures, noting that organizational unlearning can occur not only so as to allow the absorption of new knowledge, but also as a result of abandoning practices that are not fit for purpose. Tsang gives the example of abandoning the practice of securing external references in the recruit-ment of senior executives, because they provide little useful information. In this example, no new practice is introduced and the organization is purposefully accepting the unlearning of an unproductive practice.

Through the process of forgetting or unlearning, organizations are embracing ignorance and thereby recognizing the limits of their own knowledge. In some instances, unlearning and the regaining of igno-rance will enhance the scope for learning new knowledge. In other cases, abandoning existing knowledge in the form of unproductive routines and practices reduces the burden on existing cognitive capaci-ties and offers potential for resources to be allocated more productively elsewhere in the organization.

Conclusion

From this chapter it is clear that ignorance and the unknown require from management attention that goes beyond mere efforts to eliminate ignorance through learning and through new knowledge production. Within organizations, ignorance may be used in various ways, for instance to economize on cognitive resources through specialization or to stimulate innovation. In the external environment, business organiza-tions seek to manage the ignorance of their competitors through trade secrets and the exploitation of customers' ignorance, by supplying products and services designed to allow these customers either to over-come or to live happily with their own ignorance. Indeed ignorance can be used as a strategic ploy to retain and develop markets.

Purposefully incorporating ignorance into management strategies requires a new way of thinking about organization and about knowledge management. For management scholars, a greater emphasis on challeng-ing current knowledge, unlearning, forgetting, and openness to the unknown is necessary. Managers need to adopt new perspectives, which involve both a willingness to tolerate organizational ignorance where it offers possible benefits and renewed efforts to consider it where it holds latent negative outcomes. Also required is a readiness to manage the benefits and the costs of ignorance – which, although beyond comprehen-sion at one given time, may be revealed at any other. Managers need to develop strategies that explore and nurture their capacity to expect the unexpected. For knowledge managers, this requires looking beyond the knowledge that can be identified within the organization and recognizing the limits of knowledge itself and of its management. A valuable addition to the capacities of knowledge managers would be an understanding of when and how knowledge management practices can lead to ignorance through the creation of barriers to new knowledge, or of where ignorance would require efforts to generate contingency measures.

Acknowledging the potential value of organizational ignorance paves the way for its active management. For instance, although ignorance can be a barrier to innovation, it can also be a source of creative possibilities. Allowing members of the organization to expose their ignorance without fear of ridicule or prejudice facilitates experimentation, which, while it may result in failure in the short term, can lead to learning and can provide the basis for future innovations. In organizational activity focused on stimulating creativity, management strategies that encourage the exposure of ignorance by allowing ill-informed questioning may prove to give a valuable stimulus to novel thinking. Developing organizational spaces and cultures open to experimentation, resilient to failure, and that recognize ignorance as a resource repays the effort. Knowledge managers have sought to capture the knowledge of organizational members in databases and by sharing experiences with colleagues. Sharing ignorance would appear, at least on the surface, to be undesirable. However, by sharing knowledge of ignorance within organizations, one can make strategic decisions on what knowledge to prioritize and what ignorance to tolerate.

Moreover, recognizing ignorance and identifying its characteristics and sources may be just as valuable to the success of an organization as managing existing knowledge is. Different types and sources of ignorance require different management approaches, which themselves offer scope for diverse outcomes. Awareness of the various types of ignorance is the first step towards developing techniques to manage the unknown. Knowing what is not known can be as important to organizational performance as knowing what is known. A central challenge to any attempt to manage the unknown is how to achieve a balance between the negative and the positive outcomes of all the various forms of ignorance. Different management approaches may be required in different parts of an organization, and differences will exist depending on the characteristics of an organization, such as its size and its sector.

To reveal and employ ignorance, scholars and managers need to question their current knowledge and frames of reference and to embrace the unknown (Antonacopoulou, 2009). An ignorance perspective embraces change and questions stability. Rather than seeking to capture and codify knowledge, an ignorance approach recognizes the importance of unknowns and seeks to allow knowledge and ignorance to intermingle in productive and challenging ways. Every knowledge manager should be open to the unknown; for a comprehensive knowledge management strategy requires recognition of the value and pervasiveness of ignorance in organizational contexts.

7

Conclusion: Looking Forward

Forerun thy peers, thy time, and let

Thy feet, millenniums hence, be set

In midst of knowledge, dream'd not yet.

Lord Alfred Tennyson

In this very short introductory book I have sought to reflect the mainstream understandings of knowledge management. Of course, this has been done at the expense of interpretations that are currently more peripheral. Importantly, then, this text cannot be taken as a fully comprehensive account of knowledge management; rather its focus is on the dominant themes present in the academic and practitioner literature. Consequently, this book is written largely from a western perspective on knowledge management. While eastern concepts, such as *ba*, have been touched upon, this is merely a reflection of the most prominent eastern influences on the mainstream knowledge management literature. It is important to recognize this bias and therefore to acknowledge that this book is a reflection of, as well as a contribution to, the hegemony of western management knowledge. Once readers recognize the western bias in mainstream knowledge management literature and are equipped with the knowledge I have sought to impart in the pages of this book, I hope that they will be motivated to explore knowledge and its management in a range of non-western contexts and from a variety of cultural perspectives.

In this final chapter I will touch briefly on diversity as a subject that is underrepresented in mainstream considerations of knowledge management. I will also consider the future of knowledge management, and in particular the challenges that arise from the task of managing the enormous amounts of information that the multiplicity of digital communication technologies generates. In relation to this set of problems, I will underline the path-dependent nature of the codification of knowledge, and I will highlight the potential erosion of privacy and the societal damage that might arise from excessive data collection.

▉▉▉▉ Diversity: opportunities and challenges

Issues that arise from diversity need to be recognized at various levels in discussions of knowledge management as well as in the implementation of knowledge management strategies and practices. Diversity is present within organizations even in one single national context. The uneven distribution of knowledge and skills within the organization is an example of diversity among the workforce; but, importantly, diversity also exists in terms of race, class, gender, or age. Bringing together divergent perspectives can stimulate creativity (Chapter 5), yet knowledge transfer between individuals with diverse backgrounds can at the same time be challenging (Chapter 4). As Nooteboom (2009) argues, a certain degree of cognitive proximity is required for individuals to engage productively, but the existence of a degree of difference can create the cognitive dissonance required for creativity. As a result, it is important to recognize the existence of differences between those involved in the creation, acquisition, retention, and transfer of knowledge, and also to leverage such differences when they offer opportunities for knowledge creation. On the one hand, recognizing the knowledge capabilities that individuals have ensures that managers are able to utilize their skills to maximum effect within the organization. On the other hand, it is vital to note where difference may raise barriers to the creation and circulation of knowledge within organizations. The diversity of a group's membership may be too great to allow productive engagement; or, for some members, discriminatory practices may raise obstacles to the acquisition of knowledge.

Discrimination based on a range of characteristics is outlawed in many countries. In the United Kingdom, for instance, the 2010 Equality Act protects people against discrimination based on race, gender, disability, sexual orientation, religion, and age. However, discrimination is not always overt and may be deeply embedded in social norms and practices. Given the socially situated character of knowledge, it is essential to recognize that social contexts reflect differences of all sorts and that these differences lead to disparities in the abilities of organizational members to influence how knowledge is created, held, shared, and valued. Susan Durbin's (2011) discussion of the influence of gender differences on creating knowledge through networks provides a useful illustration of how barriers to knowledge creation and sharing can arise from diversity. Differentiating between formal and informal networks, Durbin highlights that senior women are often excluded from strategic informal networks, such as the old boys' network. Yet it is in these informal networks that crucial tacit knowledge is frequently shared. If women do not have access to them, their capacity for knowledge creation is impaired by comparison to the capacities of men in equivalent positions. Moreover, differential access to knowledge creates asymmetries and is a source of power for those with privileged access. Gender, race, disability, sexual orientation, religion, and age differences are not well understood in relation to knowledge management. Nevertheless, managers and scholars should recognize the opportunities and the challenges of managing diversity in relation to knowledge, both within organizations and during engagement with customers and suppliers.

Restrictions of space preclude an exhaustive examination of the topic of cultural difference. However, given that in the contemporary glo-balized business environment, most organizations must deal with cross-cultural issues in relation to their markets and/or their workforce, it is worth touching on cultural differences that do influence knowledge management, not least in terms of understandings of knowledge. For example, Robin Snell and Jacky Hong (2011) argue that, in Asian soci-eties characterized by 'collectivist' cultures, there are three cultural practices that are especially relevant for organizational learning: *guanxi* networks – that is, personal connections that can act as a resource or as a barrier; the possession of privileged knowledge as a source and sym-bol of power; and paternalistic leadership. All of these practices have implications for how knowledge is acquired, retained, and transferred in Asian as opposed to western contexts, which are predominantly characterized by 'individualist' cultures with a greater propensity for questioning authority.

Even among countries that display similar cultural characteristics, there remain differences that influence their knowledge-sharing behav-iour. For example, Snejina Michailova and Kate Hutchings (2006) find that vertical 'collectivism' and particularistic social relations in China and Russia lead to intensive social relations among organizational members, facilitating knowledge sharing between in-group members of organiza-tions in both countries. However, they also find that differences in the essence and extent of 'collectivism' in the two countries lead to different intensities of knowledge sharing in Chinese and Russian organizations. Understanding such cross-cultural differences is particularly important for knowledge managers in multinational corporations; and it is for this reason that international business scholars are increasingly active in the exploration of knowledge management in multinational contexts.

Throughout this book we have seen that knowledge is a source of power for individuals and groups as well as for organizations. Withholding knowledge, for instance through trade secrets, can be a source of market power. The power that knowledge offers can be exerted at a cultural level and across national borders. For example, through their activities in a range of national contexts, multinational corporations actively engage in the dissemination of knowledge. Given the historical development of multinational corporations in the West, it is no surprise that, in their international activities, they favour western rational approaches to knowledge and its protection over various other perspectives. Moreover, western multinational corporations employ their commercial power to appropriate and commodify knowledge developed and held by communities in countries with poorly developed intellectual property regimes; examples include the appropriation of traditional medicines and seed varieties from industrializing countries. In western assessments of knowledge, the scientist is valued above the shaman; rational knowledge is privileged over intuitive or spiritual knowledge. The spread of western multinational corporations in the twentieth century ensured the dissemination and hegemony of western management knowledge (Mir et al., 2008), a phenomenon that builds on the earlier diffusion of western knowledge through colonialism. Yet the cultural diversity of the contemporary global business environment requires variety in management approaches, not least in the field of knowledge management. The rise of multinational corporations from countries such as Brazil and China is beginning to challenge the dominance of western management knowledge, including that of knowledge management practices. Hopefully the dominance of the western perspective will soon give way to a plurality of cultural perspectives on knowledge management, to an appreciation of difference in all its various forms, and to an awareness of how the power derived from difference can be harnessed for the benefit of all.

The future of knowledge management

The very idea that knowledge can be managed is the product of a western perspective. As we have seen, early knowledge management was focused on the codification of knowledge with the assistance of computer technologies. Recognition of the limitations of this approach led to an increased emphasis on the management of knowledge in practice, as exemplified by the rise of the communities of practice approach in the late 1990s. In a sense, the turn to practice in knowledge management reflected a move away from the purely western rational approach, in which knowledge is characterized by the Cartesian separation of body and mind, towards a broader view of knowledge as embedded in the body and realized through action – an outlook that can resonate with an eastern perspective. However, the recent rise of big data has the potential to return knowledge management, through codification, to dominance. We are once again witnessing the deterministic nature of technology, which is focusing our attention on certain ways of viewing knowledge to the detriment of other possibilities. It is vital to resist a wholesale shift to knowledge management through the manipulation of codified knowledge. Computers and the algorithms that are used to analyse the data are highly valuable; but they represent particular ways of viewing the data that only create certain types of knowledge. Once established, systems of codification become difficult to alter. In this way, as I argued over a decade ago (Roberts, 2001), the excessive codification of knowledge leads to path dependence.

An example drawn from the recent book *Big Data* by Mayer-Schönberger and Cukier (2013) illustrates the potential for path dependence if all the commercial benefits of extensive data collection and analysis are taken up. According to the authors, Amazon's Kindle e-book reader has the capacity to collect data on the annotations and underlinings that its readers make to their e-books. They go on to argue:

> Marketers would love to learn which passages are most popular and use that knowledge to sell books better. Authors might like to know where in their lofty tomes most readers give up, and could use that information to improve their work. Publishers might spot themes that herald the next big book. (Mayer-Schönberger and Cukier, 2013: 132–3)

Fortunately Amazon is not (yet!) using the data that Kindle provides to assist marketers, authors, and publishers. One can speculate on the future of book publishing if such data were made available. Commercial publishers' drive for profit would lead to an intensification of the focus on the publication of books that meet all the criteria for success according to a formula derived from the data. This would result in the marginalization and (perhaps) eventual obliteration of novelty and of 'unpopular' topics. Readers would be supplied with more of the same, because this is what the data determine that they want. But is it? Memorable books are often those that challenge our accepted norms. Just because most readers give up on the more challenging literature, should we all be denied access to such work?

The codification of reading habits through the collection of data derived from e-readers seeks to remove the ambiguity of who reads what, when, and how. Yet it is the ambiguity and the uncertainty inherent in the non-codified expression of knowledge that offer enormous opportunity for novelty and creativity. There are many diverse patterns of reading, and those adopted by individuals change over time and place; they may be the result of serendipity, spontaneity, or even irrational choices. It is important to remember that the computers and the programs they operate are restricted by the imagination of those who create them, and that therefore they embed certain worldviews. If not resisted, the application of technology can lead to a narrow delineation of what represents valuable knowledge, which would have consequences for the range of products and services available – and ultimately for the type of society we live in.

We need to recognize that all forms of knowledge are valuable. Knowledge management approaches focused on the capture of codified knowledge are important; and so are approaches focused on identifying and cultivating knowing in practice. Privileging one form of knowledge management over another risks reducing the effectiveness with which knowledge as a whole is managed. Moreover, the optimum balance between these two types of knowledge management approach will vary from situation to situation. The corresponding forms of knowledge management are not only important, but also interdependent. The dichotomy explicit–tacit, which suggests that knowledge can be managed either through databases or in practice, is an oversimplification. Most knowledge work involves a combination of the explicit and the tacit; even when work focuses on explicit codified knowledge, we draw on tacit understandings to interpret it.

As we have seen in the pages of this book, knowledge management as a discipline and practice has undergone significant development during the last 25 years. It has adapted to the evolving environment and has responded to academic and practitioner criticism. Early sources of criticism, which remain relevant today, related to the broad scope of knowledge management and its lack of definitional precision (Demarest, 1997). It is for this reason that knowledge management has been described as a management fashion or fad. Moreover, it has been argued that the rise of knowledge management in the 1990s was merely a rebranding of information systems management (Wilson, 2002), and for many organizations it still revolves around the use of technology to collect and collate information. While scholarly discussions of knowledge management persist, as reflected in the continuing growth in academic publications on the topic, interest among consultants and professional service firms has been in decline for some years (Wilson, 2002; Hislop, 2010). Whether this indicates a decline in the use of knowledge management techniques in practice is debatable for, as Wiig (1997) predicted, knowledge management has perhaps become a generalized practice integrated into the general operations of organizations.

However, if knowledge management is concerned with managing every aspect of the organization, why does it remain a distinctive part of academic and practitioner discourse? One possibility is that is serves a valuable role by unifying disparate activities – from human resource management to innovation and R&D management. By offering a lens through which to see the organization as a whole, knowledge management can cut across a range of organizational practices and departments, offering a unique position for the review of an organization's performance. At an academic level, knowledge management as a discipline allows the interaction between disparate but related fields – like organization studies, human resources management, innovation studies, R&D management, and information systems management.

Knowledge management, like knowledge itself, is open to multiple interpretations. As a result, it can remain popular even though the nature of the knowledge management practices displayed in a variety of organizations is far from homogenous. We have seen in this short book that knowledge management can range from the high-tech harvesting and manipulation of data to the development of communities of practice with knowledge shared in socially situated contexts. Different knowledge activities lend themselves to different forms of management and, within any one organization, there is often a great variety of knowledge activity that requires a range of different management methods. For knowledge managers, the difficult task is to find the right balance between practices that can maximize the acquisition, retention, transfer, and creation of knowledge across their organization. Given the significance of knowledge to the economy of the twenty-first century, there remain further benefits to be gained from the appropriate management of knowledge. So, despite the persistence of certain critiques, knowledge management remains popular as a practice and as an academic discipline. From a practitioner perspective, management executives rank knowledge management as the most important potential source of increased productivity (Economist Intelligence Unit, 2006). From an academic perspective, there are vested interests in maintaining the field of knowledge management. Over the past 25 years the discipline has become self-sustaining through an expanding number of academic journals (see Appendix), conferences, research centres, and degree programmes and modules focused on knowledge management.

Yet the extent to which knowledge as a whole can be efficiently managed remains open to question. And if knowledge cannot be managed efficiently, efforts focused specifically on it may waste resources and ultimately be counterproductive. For instance, in fast-changing environments, certain forms of knowledge may quickly become outdated, so efforts to capture them through codification are redundant even prior to completion. Furthermore, efforts to pin down the meaning of knowledge in a form that can be captured and retained, whether in databases or in communities, contribute to the ossification of knowledge and management structures; and this results in a reduction of flexibility, which is a key source of competitiveness. It is this tendency for certain knowledge to become accepted as the norm that can lead to organizational rigidities. This is why major organizational crises often require the removal of top managers: with them dominant ideas and accepted knowledge practices are also removed.

What does the future hold for knowledge workers? Focused on organizational efficiency, innovation, and creative capacities, knowledge management is often promoted as a positive development for workers, because it offers them greater autonomy. Yet knowledge management can result in the intensification of surveillance and in the further deskilling of workers. Moreover, knowledge management practices can promote the commodification of the cognitive capacities of the workforce. Adopting a Marxist-informed perspective, Phil Graham argues: 'In the knowledge economy, products of human cognition simultaneously become the primary source of surplus-value, the primary means of production, and the primary *object* of production' (2006: 74). From this perspective, knowledge management is more than a manifestation and intensification of previous management practices developed in the Taylorist tradition. While scientific management sought to maximize the value obtained from the physical labour of workers, the focus in a knowledge economy is on the minds of workers – since the creative cognitive capacities of knowledge workers came to be of central commercial value to businesses. Profits derive from the commodification and appropriation of human cognition. Moreover, for many high-skilled knowledge workers, there is little or no distinction between work and free time. They are as likely to cogitate about a work-based problem in their free time, among family or friends, as they would at their desk in an office. The separation between work and leisure becomes increasingly blurred.

It is evident that organizations not only appropriate the knowledge of their employees, but increasingly seek to exploit the knowledge held by their suppliers and customers. This is particularly true where customer communities support marketing and innovation activities. For example, in the mobile telephone sector, companies like Nokia support and interact with a range of online user groups in order to acquire knowledge about their own products and how they might be developed to meet customer needs better. In the era of the Internet and social media, all those who engage with tools like Google, Facebook, Twitter, and YouTube are producing knowledge content that may be appropriated by business organizations for commercial purposes; are being exposed to advertising; or are having their usage patterns analysed with a view to producing commercially useful data. In the digital world almost everything we do leaves a trail of data that, when analysed, can generate commercially valuable knowledge. Information about us is constantly collected and collated by businesses and state agencies in order to generate knowledge of our personal communications, patterns of Internet browsing, geographical movements, purchasing habits. State security agencies use such knowledge to prevent acts of terrorism – or, in states where democracy is under threat or absent, to crush opposition. Businesses apply the knowledge they have gathered in various ways – for instance in marketing, where they ensure that we are exposed to the latest advertisement or sponsored link for a product or service that we are likely to purchase (according to our 'data profile'). If you have a Google e-mail account, you will have experienced the bespoke advertising that results from the analysis of your e-mails. When I first opened a Gmail account, I was surprised to see the appearance, on my inbox page, of adverts for boating holidays on the Norfolk Broads shortly after I had sent an e-mail about visiting a relative in Norfolk. As we enter the era of big data, we can expect an intensification of the harvesting of our online communications for commercial and governance purposes.

In the age of the Internet and social media we have become so accustomed to surveillance that, when the news broke in June 2013 of the US National Security Agency (NSA)'s clandestine electronic surveillance programme, PRISM – which collects and stores vast quantities of global e-mail messages, Facebook posts, Internet histories, and telephone calls – no major popular upsurge occurred. Nevertheless, we must be aware of the threats to privacy and freedom that such surveillance presents, and therefore of the need for a regulation of the scale and scope of data collection activity. In Chapter 2 I mentioned the Domesday Book as an early example of the management of data. The fact that the survey of property ownership initiated by William the Conqueror in 1086 became known as 'the Domesday Book' was a reflection of people's concerns about the nature of the information collected about them, the uses to which it might have been put, and – of course – its accuracy. In today's world, concerns about the collection of data are rather muted. Surely we should take note of these early worries and reflect seriously on the dangers of the mass data harvesting that is currently occurring through social media sites like Facebook.

However, rather than questioning the intensification of data collection, we are actually contributing to it, as many of us develop our own systems of managing the information and the knowledge that are important to us. In the current era, personal data collection goes beyond the diaries, address books, and music, photo, and video archives that individuals maintain to record their lives and their family and social networks. We are, to a greater or lesser extent – depending on our level of obsession and purpose – increasingly collecting knowledge about ourselves and our lives by using wearable technologies or by activating smartphone applications to gather data on distances walked, calories consumed, weight, blood pressure, quality of sleep, and so on. Some lead-users of such technologies are wearing products like the Google Glass and the Narrative Clip (a lifelogging camera) to capture almost every moment of their lives.

Clearly, access to the vast quantities of data that are currently being produced offers the potential to develop knowledge of huge benefit for business and society. Those seeking to solve problems are now able to draw on an enormous body of information and ideas. The combination of codification and computing power assists in the creation of new knowledge, enabling the analysis of information in ways that were previously unimaginable. One of the most prominent examples of the advantages of combining computing power with huge amounts of data is the decoding of DNA in the human genome project and the subsequent advances in medical research and treatments.

In light of the opportunities presented by the ever-increasing quantities of data, the management of knowledge is likely to continue to offer potential for productivity gains. The analysis of vast amounts of data yields the knowledge foundations required for the development of new products and services. Of course, the development of new knowledge and understanding does not necessarily lead to change. As you will remember, in Chapter 1 the idea of knowledge as power was noted. This correlation is relevant at an individual level, where power can influence the extent to which knowledge is shared; and it also occurs in the competitive activity between business organizations when the withholding of knowledge through trade secrets offers market power. It is also important to note that power itself can influence knowledge: it can determine what knowledge is available and what knowledge is suppressed. The power of vested interests can prevent the dissemination of knowledge that threatens those interests; or, where dissemination occurs, power can be deployed to discredit such knowledge. The debate over global warming is a useful illustration of how power can be deployed to discredit knowledge. Despite the evidence of global warming that has been accumulating over the last 40 years, it is only very recently that those with vested interests in fossil fuels, including large oil companies, have been less resistant to recognizing the validity of the scientific knowledge claims and the need for policymakers to act on this knowledge.

Power lends the resources needed to stifle research into the development of knowledge in certain areas as well as to suppress undesirable or harmful knowledge. While there may be a place for the suppression of knowledge for moral or social reasons – for example, knowledge of how to create a nuclear bomb – and states may be justified in preventing the dissemination of such knowledge, suppression merely for commercial purposes cannot always be justified in terms of the social good. A classic example from the past is the suppression and discrediting, achieved by the large tobacco companies in the 1950s and early 1960s, of evidence of the link between tobacco smoking and lung cancer. It is therefore vital to recognize both the power that knowledge can give and the fact that power can influence what knowledge is made available and recognized as legitimate and valuable. Scholars of knowledge management need to make further efforts to understand the relationship between knowledge and power in organizations, as well as to recognize that the suppression of knowledge involves the active construction of ignorance. Consequently the management of knowledge can give rise to questions concerning the ethics of business practice.

The way forward?

Knowledge management is an established field of academic study and a management practice that continues to be valued by academics and managers alike. In looking to the future development of the field, it is important to recognize the potential influence of digital technologies and the phenomenon of big data. We must also acknowledge the dangers that a primary focus on codified knowledge can represent, both in terms of path dependency and from a societal perspective. It is natural to focus on the forms of knowledge that we understand and that fit nicely with our methods of analysis. However, the knowledge we consciously possess is possibly only a small amount of the knowledge we can potentially access. Intuition gives us an indication that we know much more than we take ourselves to know. Incorporating intuition, and even spiritual aspects of knowledge, may offer additional opportunities to understand knowledge. Indeed, as Chapter 6 underlined, we need to be open to the unknown – we hold knowledge of which we are unaware, and there is knowledge yet to be discovered.

We need to explore knowledge in a wider context and to go beyond western perspectives that prioritize rationality. Rather an approach that incorporates the unknown, the irrational, and even the spiritual may offer fresh potential for understanding knowledge and its management.

Eastern philosophical traditions may provide rich resources from which to draw in future explorations of knowledge. The race to appropriate knowledge, to exert ownership over it, and thereby to subsume it to the market has been a feature of western economic development and has intensified with the rise of neoliberalism since the late 1970s. Indeed this trend is captured by the very expressions 'knowledge economy' and 'knowledge management'. However, the focus on knowledge that can be owned and commodified has resulted in the neglect of a broader spectrum of knowledge. While the neglected knowledge does not have commercial value per se, this is no reason to ignore or discard it. The sociocultural value of knowledge must be acknowledged; for we must remember that business transactions exist and are underpinned by sociocultural phenomena, for instance by communities and by trust. Similarly, commercial knowledge exists on a foundation in which knowledge is embedded in sociocultural contexts. We can look to the future for the knowledge 'dream'd not yet' of Lord Alfred Tennyson's line (which opens this chapter); but if we open our eyes to perceive knowledge in all its various forms, perhaps we will not have to wait for millennia to enjoy a vast extension in our knowledge resources.

References

Adler, P.S. (2001). 'Market, hierarchy, and trust: The knowledge economy and the future of capitalism'. *Organization Science* 12 (2): 215–34.

Akerlof, G.A. (1970). 'The market for "lemons": Qualitative uncertainty and the market mechanism'. *Quarterly Journal of Economics* 84: 488–500.

Alge, B.J., Ballinger, G.A., Tangirala, S. and Oakley, J.L. (2006). 'Information privacy in organizations: Empowering creative and extra role performance'. *Journal of Applied Psychology* 91 (1): 221–32.

Alonso, M.F. (2007). 'Can we protect traditional knowledge?' In B. de Sousa Santos (ed.), *Another Knowledge is Possible: Beyond Northern Epistemologies*, pp. 249–71. London: Verso.

Alvesson, M. and Karreman, D. (2001). 'Odd couple: Making sense of the curious concept of knowledge management'. *Journal of Management Studies* 38 (7): 995–1018.

Amabile, T.M. (1997). 'Motivating creativity in organizations: On doing what you love and loving what you do'. *California Management Review* 40 (1): 39–58.

Amabile, T.M. (1998). 'How to kill creativity'. *Harvard Business Review* 76 (5): 77–87.

American Productivity and Quality Centre (APQC) (2014). *Knowledge Management Glossary*. Huston: APQC. At www.apqc.org/knowledge-base/download/320028/K05406_KM_kmglossary.pdf (accessed 18 September 2014).

Amin, A. (1994). *Post-Fordism: A Reader*. Oxford: Blackwell.

Amin, A. and Roberts, J. (2008). 'Knowing in action: Beyond communities of practice'. *Research Policy* 37 (2): 353–69.

Anderson, C. (2008). *The Long Tail: Why the Future of Business Is Selling Less of More*, revised edn. New York: Hyperion.

Antonacopoulou, E.P. (2009). 'Knowledge impact and scholarship: Unlearning and practising to co-create actionable'. *Management Learning* 40 (1): 421–30.

Argote, L. (2013). *Organizational Learning: Creating, Retaining and Transferring Knowledge*. New York: Springer.

Argyris, C. and Schön, D. (1978). *Organizational Learning: A Theory of Action Perspective*. Reading, MA: Addison-Wesley.

Arrow, K.J. (1962). 'The economic implications of learning by doing'. *The Review of Economic Studies* 29 (3): 155–73.

Arrow, K.J. (1969). 'Classificatory notes on the production and transmission of technological knowledge'. *The American Economic Review* 59 (2): 29–35.

Arrow, K.J. (1974). *The Limits of Organization.* New York: W. W. Norton.

Barney, J.B. (1991). 'Firm resources and sustained competitive advantage'. *Journal of Management* 17 (1): 99–120.

Bassi, L. (1999). 'Harnessing the power of intellectual capital'. In J. Cortada and J. Woods (eds), *The Knowledge Management Year Book, 1999–2000*, pp. 422–31. Boston, MA: Butterworth Heinemann.

BBC (2010). 'Deepwater disaster: The untold story'. *Horizon*, 16 November 2010, BBC 2. At www.bbc.co.uk/programmes/b00w5qs8 (accessed 20 March 2012).

Bell, D. (1974). *The Coming of Post-Industrial Society.* London: Heinemann.

Benkler, Y. (2006). *The Wealth of Networks: How Social Production Transforms Markets and Freedom.* New Haven, CT and London: Yale University Press.

Better Off Ted (2009). 'Battle of the bulbs'. Episode 3, Series 2. ABC network, USA.

Bilton, C. (2007). *Management and Creativity: From Creative Industries to Creative Management.* Oxford: Wiley Blackwell.

Blackler, F. (1995). 'Knowledge, knowledge work and organizations: An overview and interpretation'. *Organization Studies* 16 (6): 1021–46.

Boden, M.A. (2004). *The Creative Mind: Myths and Mechanisms*, 2nd edn. London: Routledge.

Boisot, M.H. (1998). *Knowledge Assets: Securing Competitive Advantage in the Information Economy.* Oxford: Oxford University Press.

Boldrin, M. and Levine, D.K. (2008). *Against Intellectual Monopoly.* New York: Cambridge University Press.

Boutellier, R., Grassmann, O., Macho, H. and Roux, M. (1998). 'Management of dispersed product development teams: The role of information technologies'. *R&D Management* 28: 13–25.

Bowles, S. and Gintis, H. (2002). 'Social capital and community governance'. *The Economic Journal* 112: F419–F436.

Bradshaw, T. and Mundy, S. (2012). 'Apple battle with Samsung moves to US court'. *Financial Times*, 29 July. At www.ft.com/cms/s/0/f85d4694-d994-11e1-a18e-00144feab49a.html#axzz2TkpoBgEf (accessed 13 July 2014).

Braverman, H. (1974). *Labor and Monopoly Capital.* New York: Monthly Review Press.

Brown, J. (2010). 'Cashing in, the couple who dreamed up Tesco Clubcard'. *The Independent,* Tuesday 17 August. At www. independent.co.uk/news/people/profiles/cashing-in-the-couple-who-dreamed-up-tesco-clubcard-2054543.html (accessed 13 July 2014).

Brown, J.S. and Duguid, P. (1991). 'Organizational learning and communities of practice: Towards a unified view of working, learning and innovation'. *Organization Science* 2: 40–57.

Brown, J.S. and Duguid, P. (2001). 'Knowledge and organization: A social-practice perspective'. *Organization Science* 12 (2): 198–213.

Caldwell, L.K. (1967). 'Managing the scientific super-culture: The task of educational preparation'. *Public Administration Review* 27 (2): 128–33.

Cangelosi, V.E. and Dill, W.R. (1965). 'Organizational learning: Observations towards a theory'. *Administrative Science Quarterly* 10 (2): 175–203.

Carroll, J.D. and Henry, N. (1975). 'A symposium: Knowledge management'. *Public Administration Review* 35 (6): 616–38.

Casson, M. (1997). *Information and Organization: A New Perspective on the Theory of the Firm.* Oxford: Clarendon Press.

Castells, M. (1996). *The Information Age: Economy, Society and Culture,* volume 1: *The Rise of the Network Society.* Oxford: Blackwell.

Chandler, A.D., Jr (1962). *Strategy and Structure: Chapters in the History of the American Industrial Enterprise.* Cambridge, MA: MIT Press.

Chandler, A.D., Jr (1977). *The Visible Hand: The Managerial Revolution in American Business.* Cambridge, MA: Harvard University Press.

Chesbrough, H.W. (2006). *Open Innovation: The New Imperative for Creating and Profiting from Technology.* Cambridge, MA: Harvard Business School Press.

Coase, R. (1937). 'The nature of the firm'. *Economica* 4 (16): 386–405.

Coe, N.M. and Bunnell, T.G. (2003). '"Spatializing" knowledge communities: Towards a conceptualisation of transnational innovation networks'. *Global Networks* 3 (4): 437–56.

Cohen, W.M. and Levinthal, D.A. (1990). 'Absorptive capacity: A new perspective on learning and innovation'. *Administrative Science Quarterly* 35 (1): 128–52.

Collins, H. (2001). 'Tacit knowledge, trust and the Q of sapphire'. *Social Studies of Science* 31 (1): 71–85.

Collins, H. (2010). *Tacit and Explicit Knowledge.* Chicago, IL: University of Chicago Press.

Cook, S. and Yanow, D. (1993). 'Culture and organizational learning'. *Journal of Management Inquiry* 2 (4): 373–90.

Cowan, R. and Foray, D. (1997). 'The economics of codification and the diffusion of knowledge'. *Industrial and Corporate Change* 6 (3): 595–622.

Cowan, R., David, P.A. and Foray, D. (2000). 'The explicit economics of knowledge codification and tacitness'. *Industrial and Corporate Change* 9 (2): 211–53.

Csikszentmihalyi, M. (1996). *Creativity: The Work and Lives of 91 Eminent People*. New York: HarperCollins.

Cyert, R.M. and March, J.G. (1963). *A Behavioral Theory of the Firm*. Englewood Cliffs, NJ: Prentice Hall.

Davenport, T.H. and Prusak, L. (1998). *Working Knowledge: How Organizations Manage What They Know*. Boston, MA: Harvard Business School Press.

Davenport, T.H., De Long, D.W. and Beers, M.C. (1998). 'Successful knowledge management projects'. *Sloan Management Review* 40: 43–57.

Demarest, M. (1997). 'Understanding knowledge management'. *Journal of Long Range Planning* 30 (3): 374–84.

Department of Culture, Media and Sport (DCMS) (1998). *Creative Industries Mapping Document 1998*. London: DCMS.

Dewey, J. (1938). *Education and Experience*. West Lafayette, IN: Kappa Delta Pi.

The Domesday Book Online (n.d.). At www.domesdaybook.co.uk/index.html (accessed 11 July 2014).

Draft, R.L. and Weick, K.L. (1984). 'Towards a model of organizations as interpretive systems'. *Academy of Management Review* 9 (2): 284–95.

Drucker, P.F. (1969). *The Age of Discontinuity: Guidelines to Our Changing Society*. New York: Harper & Row.

Drucker, P.F. (1993). *Post-Capitalist Society*. Oxford: Butterworth Heinemann.

Durbin, S. (2011). 'Creating knowledge through networks: A gender perspective'. *Gender, Work & Organization* 18 (1): 90–112.

Earl, M.J. and Scott, I.A. (1999). 'What is a chief knowledge officer?' *Sloan Management Review* 40 (2): 29–38.

Easterby-Smith, M. and Lyles, M.A. (eds) (2005). *The Blackwell Handbook of Organizational Learning and Knowledge Management*. Oxford: Blackwell.

Easterby-Smith, M. and Lyles, M.A. (eds) (2011). *Handbook of Organizational Learning and Knowledge Management*, 2nd edn. Chichester: John Wiley & Sons Ltd.

Easterby-Smith, M., Crossan, M. and Nicolini, D. (2000). 'Organizational learning: Debates past, present and future'. *Journal of Management Studies* 37 (6): 783–96.

Economist Intelligence Unit (EIU) (2006). *Foresight 2020: Economic, Industry and Corporate Trends*. London: Economist Intelligence Unit.

Edquist, C. (1997). 'Systems of innovation approaches: Their emergence and characteristics'. In C. Edquist (ed.), *Systems of Innovation: Technologies, Institutions and Organizations*, pp. 1–35. London: Pinter.

Eliot, T.S. (1934). *The Rock*. London: Faber & Faber.

Epple, D., Argote, L. and Devadas, R. (1991). 'Organizational learning curves: A method for investigating intra-plant transfer of knowledge acquired through learning by doing'. *Organization Science* 2 (1): 58–70.

Farivar, C. (2012). 'On the run: How the Pirate Bay founders dodged Swedish justice'. At www.wired.co.uk/news/archive/2012-10/04/how-pirate-bay-dodged-swedish-justice (accessed 13 July 2014).

Fiol, C.M. and Lyles, M.A. (1985). 'Organizational learning'. *Academy of Management Review* 10: 803–13.

Florida, R.L. (2002). *The Rise of the Creative Class*. New York: Basic Books.

Foucault, M. (1979). *Discipline and Punish: The Birth of the Prison*, trans. A. Sheridan. Harmondsworth: Penguin.

Freeman, C. (1987). *Technology Policy and Economic Performance: Lessons from Japan*. London: Pinter.

Frické, M. (2009). 'The knowledge pyramid: A critique of the DIKW hierarchy'. *Journal of Information Science* 35 (2): 13–142.

Fukuyama, F. (1995). *Trust: The Social Virtues and the Creation of Prosperity*. London: Penguin Books.

Garrat, B. (1987). *The Learning Organization*. London: Fontana.

Gherardi, S. (2006). *Organizational Knowledge: The Texture of Workplace Learning*. Oxford: Wiley Blackwell.

Gleick, J. (2011). *The Information: A History, a Theory, a Flood*. London: Fourth Estate.

Glisby, M. and Holden, N. (2003). 'Contextual constraints in knowledge management theory: The cultural embeddedness of Nonaka's knowledge creating company'. *Knowledge and Process Management* 10 (1): 29–36.

Godin, B. (2006). 'The knowledge-based economy: Conceptual framework or buzzword?' *The Journal of Technology Transfer* 31 (1): 17–30.

Gourlay, S. (2006). 'Conceptualizing knowledge creation: A critique of Nonaka's theory'. *Journal of Management Studies* 43 (7): 1415–36.

Graham, P. (2006). *Hypercapitalism: New Media, Language, and Social Perceptions of Value*. New York: Peter Lang.

Grant, R.M. (1996). 'Toward a knowledge-based theory of the firm'. *Strategic Management Journal* 17 (S2): 109–22.

Grey, C. (2013). *A Very Short, Fairly Interesting and Reasonably Cheap Book about Studying Organizations*, 3rd edn. London: Sage.

Gross, M. (2010). *Ignorance and Surprise: Science, Society, and Ecological Design*. Cambridge, MA: MIT Press.

Hansen, M.T., Nohria, N. and Tierney, T. (1999). 'What's your strategy for managing knowledge?' *Harvard Business Review* 77 (2): 106–16.

Hayes, R.H., Wheelwright, S.C. and Clark, K.B. (1988). *Dynamic Manufacturing: Creating the Learning Organization*. New York: Free Press.

Hedberg, B. (1981). 'How organizations learn and unlearn'. In P.C. Nystrom and W.H. Starbuck (eds), *Handbook of Organizational Design*, pp. 3–27. New York: Oxford University Press.

Hislop, D. (2009). *Knowledge Management in Organizations*, 2nd edn. Oxford: Oxford University Press.

Hislop, D. (2010). 'Knowledge management as an ephemeral management fashion?' *Journal of Knowledge Management* 14 (6): 779–90.

Howkins, J. (2002). *The Creative Economy: How People Make Money from Ideas*. London: Penguin Books.

Huber, G.P. (1991). 'Organizational learning: The contributing processes and the literatures'. *Organization Science* 2: 88–115.

Hull, R. (2000). 'Knowledge management practices and innovation'. In B. Andersen, J. Howells, R. Hull, I. Miles and J. Roberts (eds), *Knowledge and Innovation in the New Service Economy*, pp. 142–58. Cheltenham: Edward Elgar.

Janis, I.L. (1972). *Victims of Groupthink: A Psychological Study of Foreign-policy Decisions and Fiascoes*. Boston, MA: Houghton Mifflin.

Jensen, M.C. and Meckling, W.H. (1976). Theory of the firm: Managerial behavior, agency costs and ownership structure. *Journal of Financial Economics* 3 (4): 305–60.

Knight, F.H. (2010) [1921]. *Risk, Uncertainty and Profit*. Forgotten Books. At www.forgottenbooks.org (accessed 19 June 2010).

Knopper, S. (2009). *Appetite for Self-Destruction: The Spectacular Crash of the Record Industry in the Digital Age*. New York: Free Press.

Knorr-Cetina, K. (1999). *Epistemic Cultures: How the Sciences Make Sense*. Chicago, IL: University of Chicago Press.

Koenig, M. and Neveroski, K. (2008). 'The origins and development of knowledge management'. *Journal of Information and Knowledge Management* 7 (4): 243–54.

Koestler, A. (1976). *The Act of Creation*. London: Hutchinson.

Kruger, J. and Dunning, D. (1999). 'Unskilled and unaware of it: How difficulties of recognizing one's own incompetence lead to inflated self-assessments'. *Journal of Personality and Social Psychology* 77 (6): 1121–34.

Kuhn, T.S. (1996). *The Structure of Scientific Revolutions*, 3rd edn. Chicago, IL: University of Chicago Press.

Lambe, P. (2011). 'The unacknowledged parentage of knowledge management'. *Journal of Knowledge Management* 15 (2): 175–97.

Landes, D.S. (1999). *The Wealth and Poverty of Nations*. London: Abacus.

Lane, P.J. and Lubatkin, M. (1998). 'Relative absorptive capacity and interorganizational learning'. *Strategic Management Journal* 19 (5): 461–77.

Lave, J. and Wenger, E. (1991). *Situated Learning: Legitimate Peripheral Participation*. Cambridge: Cambridge University Press.

Lazaric, N. and Lorenz, E. (1998). 'Introduction: The learning dynamics of trust, reputation and confidence'. In N. Lazaric and E. Lorenz (eds), *Trust and Economic Learning*, pp. 1–20. Cheltenham: Edward Elgar.

Leadbeater, C. (2008). *We-Think: Mass Innovation, Not Mass Production*. London: Profile Books.

Leonard-Barton, D. (1995). *Wellsprings of Knowledge: Building and Sustaining the Sources of Innovation*. Boston, MA: Harvard University Press.

Lessig, L. (2004). *Free Culture: The Nature and Future of Creativity*. London: Penguin Books.

Liebeskind, J.P. (1997). 'Keeping organizational secrets: Protective institutional mechanisms and their costs'. *Industrial and Corporate Change* 6 (3): 623–63.

Liebowitz, J. (2008). '"Think of others" in knowledge management: Making culture work for you'. *Knowledge Management Research & Practice* 6: 47–51.

Liebowitz, J. and Wilcox, L.C. (1997). *Knowledge Management and its Integrative Elements*. Boca Raton, FL: CRC Press.

Lindkvist, L. (2005). 'Knowledge communities and knowledge collectivities: A typology of knowledge work in groups'. *Journal of Management Studies* 42 (6): 1189–210.

Longstaff, P.H. (2005). *Security, Resilience, and Communication in Unpredictable Environments Such as Terrorism, Natural Disasters, and Complex Technology*. Cambridge, MA: Center for Information Policy Research, Harvard University. At http://pirp.harvard.edu/pubs_pdf/longsta/longsta-p05-3.pdf (accessed 12 September 2014).

Loveridge, D. (2009). *Foresight: The Art and Science of Anticipating the Future.* New York: Routledge.

Lundvall, B.-Å. (1992). 'Introduction'. In B.-Å. Lundvall (ed.), *National Systems of Innovation: Towards a Theory of Innovation and Interactive Learning*, pp. 1–19. London: Pinter.

Machlup, F. (1962). *The Production and Distribution of Knowledge in the United States.* Princeton, NJ: Princeton University Press.

MacKenzie, D. and Spinardi, G. (1995). 'Tacit knowledge, weapons design, and the uninvention of nuclear weapons'. *American Journal of Sociology* 101: 44–99.

March, J.G. (1976). 'The technology of foolishness'. In J.C. March and J.P. Olsen (eds), *Ambiguity and Choice in Organizations*, pp. 69–81. Bergen, Norway: Universitetsforlaget.

March, J.G. (1991). 'Exploration and exploitation in organizational learning'. *Organization Science* 2 (1): 71–87.

March, J.G. and Simon, H. (1993) [1958]. *Organization.* Oxford: Wiley Blackwell.

Markoff, J. and Hansell, S. (2006). 'Hiding in plain sight, Google seeks more power'. *New York Times*, 14 June. At www.nytimes.com/2006/06/14/technology/14search.html?pagewanted=all&_r (accessed 11 July 2014).

Marshall, A. (1890). *Principles of Economics.* London: Macmillan Press.

Martin de Holan, P. and Phillips, N. (2004). 'Remembrance of things past? The dynamics of organizational forgetting'. *Management Science* 50 (11): 1603–13.

Mayer-Schönberger, V. and Cukier, K. (2013). *Big Data: A Revolution That Will Transform How We Live, Work and Think.* London: John Murray.

McKenna, B. (2005). 'Wisdom, ethics and postmodern organization'. In D. Rooney, G. Hearn and A. Ninan (eds), *Handbook on the Knowledge Economy*, pp. 37–53. Cheltenham: Edward Elgar.

Michailova, S. and Hutchings, K. (2006). 'National cultural influences on knowledge sharing: A comparison of China and Russia'. *Journal of Management Studies* 43 (3): 383–405.

Mir, R., Banerjee, S.B. and Mir, A. (2008). 'Hegemony and its discontents: A critical analysis of organizational knowledge transfer'. *Critical Perspectives on International Business* 4 (2/3): 203–27.

Mirvis, P.H. (1996). 'Historical foundations of organization learning'. *Journal of Organizational Change Management* 9 (1): 13–31.

Mokyr, J. (2002). *The Gifts of Athena: Historical Origins of the Knowledge Economy.* Princeton, NJ: Princeton University Press.

Nelson, R. and Winter, S. (1982). *An Evolutionary Theory of Economic Change.* Cambridge, MA: Harvard University Press.

Nonaka, I. and Konno, N. (1998). 'The concept of "Ba": Building a foundation for knowledge creation'. *California Management Review* 40 (3): 40–54.

Nonaka, I. and Takeuchi, H. (1995). *The Knowledge-Creating Company: How Japanese Companies Create the Dynamics of Innovation*. Oxford: Oxford University Press.

Nooteboom, B. (2009). *A Cognitive Theory of the Firm: Learning, Governance and Dynamic Capabilities*. Cheltenham: Edward Elgar.

Nystrom, P.C. and Starbuck, W.H. (1984). 'To avoid organizational crises, unlearn'. *Organizational Dynamics* 12 (4): 53–65.

OECD (1996). *The Knowledge-based Economy*. Paris: OECD.

O'Leary, D. (1998). 'Using AI in knowledge management: Knowledge bases and ontologies'. *IEEE Intelligent Systems* 13: 34–9.

Oram, A. and Wilson, G. (2007). *Beautiful Code: Leading Programmers Explain How They Think*. Sebastopol, CA: O'Reilly Media.

Orr, J.E. (1996). *Talking about Machines: An Ethnography of a Modern Job*. Ithaca, NY: IRL Press/Cornell University Press.

Oxford Dictionary of English (ODE) (2003). Oxford: Oxford University Press.

Penrose, E. (1959). *Theory of the Growth of the Firm*. New York: Wiley.

Polanyi, M. (1966). 'The logic of tacit inference'. *Philosophy* 41 (155): 1–18.

Polanyi, M. (1967). *The Tacit Dimension*. London: Routledge.

Polanyi, M. (1958). *Personal Knowledge: Towards a Post-Critical Philosophy*. London: Routledge and Kegan Paul.

Popper, K. (2004) [1963]. *Conjectures and Refutations: The Growth of Scientific Knowledge*. London: Routledge.

Porat, M. (1977). *The Information Economy: Definition and Measurement*. Office of Telecommunications report. Washington, DC: US Department of Commerce.

Powell, W.W. and Snellman, K. (2004). 'The knowledge economy'. *Annual Review of Sociology* 30: 199–220.

Proctor, R.N. (2008). 'Agnotology: A missing term to describe the cultural production of ignorance (and its study)'. In R.N. Proctor and L. Schiebinger (eds), *Agnotolology: The Making and Unmaking of Ignorance*, pp. 1–33. Stanford, CA: Stanford University Press.

Prusak, L. and Matson, E. (2006). *Knowledge Management and Organizational Learning: A Reader*. Oxford: Oxford University Press.

Putnam, R.D. (2000). *Bowling Alone: The Collapse and Revival of American Community*. New York: Simon and Schuster.

Rainey, S. (2013). 'Nick D'Aloiso: "It was a massive gamble but a good one"'. *The Telegraph*, 26 March. At www.telegraph.co.uk/apps/9954896/Nick-DAloiso-It-was-a-massive-gamble-but-a-good-one.html (accessed 28 July 2014).

Rigby, D.K. (2011). *Management Tools 2011: An Executive's Guide*. Boston, MA: Bain & Company. At www.bain.com/Images/Bain_Management_Tools_2011.pdf (accessed 27 August 2014).

Rigby, D.K. and Bilodeau, B. (2009). *Management Tools and Trends 2009*. Boston, MA: Bain & Company.

Roberts, J. (1998). *Multinational Business Service Firms: The Development of Multinational Organisational Structures in the UK Business Services Sector*. Aldershot: Ashgate.

Roberts, J. (2000). 'From know-how to show-how? Questioning the role of information and communication technologies in knowledge transfer'. *Technology Analysis and Strategic Management* 12 (4): 429–43.

Roberts, J. (2001). 'The drive to codify: Implications for the knowledge-based economy'. *Prometheus: The Journal of Issues in Technology Change, Innovation, Information Economics, Communications and Science Policy* 19 (2): 99–116.

Roberts, J. (2003). 'Trust and electronic knowledge transfer'. *International Journal of Electronic Business* 1 (2): 168–86.

Roberts, J. (2006). 'Limits to communities of practice'. *Journal of Management Studies* 43 (3): 623–39.

Roberts, J. (2009). 'The global knowledge economy in question'. *Critical Perspectives on International Business* 5 (4): 285–303.

Roberts, J. (2013). 'Organizational ignorance: Towards a managerial perspective on the unknown?' *Management Learning* 44 (3): 215–36.

Roberts, J. and Armitage, J. (2008). 'The ignorance economy'. *Prometheus: Critical Studies in Innovation* 26 (4): 335–54.

Rogers, E. (1962). *Diffusion of Innovations*. New York: Free Press.

Rowley, J. (2007). The wisdom hierarchy: Representations of the DIKW hierarchy. *Journal of Information Science* 33 (2): 163–80.

Saint-Onge, H. and Wallace, D. (2003). *Leveraging Communities of Practice for Strategic Advantage*. London: Butterworth Heinemann.

Scarbrough, H., Swan, J. and Preston, J. (1999). *Knowledge Management: A Literature Review*. London: Chartered Institute of Personnel and Development.

Schoemaker, P. (1995). 'Scenario planning: A tool for strategic thinking'. *Sloan Management Review* 36 (2): 25–40.

Scientific American Mind (2014). 'Special collector's edition: The mad science of creativity'. *Scientific American Mind* 23 (1).

Senge, P.M. (1990). *The Fifth Discipline: The Art and Practice of the Learning Organization*. New York: Doubleday/Currency.

Sennett, R. (2008). *The Craftsman*. London and New York: Allen Lane.

Serenko, A. and Bontis, N. (2013). 'Global ranking of knowledge management and intellectual capital academic journals: 2013 update'. *Journal of Knowledge Management* 17 (2): 307–26.

Shannon, C.E. and Weaver, W. (1949). *The Mathematical Theory of Communication*. Urbana, IL: University of Illinois Press.

Sherwell, P. (2010). 'BP disaster: Worst oil spill in US history turns seas into a dead zone'. *The Telegraph*, 29 May. At www.telegraph.co.uk/finance/newsbysector/energy/oilandgas/7783656/ BP-disaster-worst-oil-spill-in-US-history-turns-seas-into-a-dead-zone.html (accessed 12 September 2014).

Shiva, V. (2007). 'Biodiversity, intellectual property rights, and globalization'. In B. de Sousa Santos (ed.), *Another Knowledge Is Possible: Beyond Northern Epistemologies*, pp. 272–88. London: Verso.

Shrivastra, P. (1983). 'A typology of organizational learning systems'. *Journal of Management Studies* 20 (1): 7–28.

Simon, H.A. (1955). 'A behavioural model of rational choice'. *Quarterly Journal of Economics* 69: 99–118.

Simon, H.A. (1973). 'Applying information technology to organizational design'. *Public Administration Review* 33 (3): 268–78.

Simon, H.A. (1991). 'Bounded rationality and organizational learning'. *Organization Science* 2 (1): 125–34.

Smith, K. (2002). 'What is the knowledge economy? Knowledge intensity and distributed knowledge bases'. UNU/INTECH Discussion Paper, The United Nations University, Institute for New Technologies, Maastricht, The Netherlands, ISSN 1564–8370. Available at: http://www.intech.unu.edu/publications/discussion-papers/2002-6.pdf (accessed 23 December 2014).

Smithson, M. (1989). *Ignorance and Uncertainty: Emerging Paradigms*. New York: Springer.

Snell, R. and Hong, J. (2011). 'Organizational learning in Asia'. In M. Easterby-Smith and M.A. Lyles (eds), *Handbook of Organizational Learning and Knowledge Management*, 2nd edn, pp. 635–58. Chichester: John Wiley & Sons Ltd.

Spender, J.-C. (1996). 'Organizational knowledge, learning and memory: Three concepts in search of a theory'. *Journal of Organizational Change Management* 9 (1): 63–78.

Stafford, L. (2011). 'Coke hides its secret formula in plain sight in World of Coca-Cola move'. *Atlanta Journal-Constitution*, 8 December. At www.ajc.com/news/business/coke-hides-its-secret-formula-in-plain-sight-in-wo/nQPMm/ (accessed 13 July 2014).

Stewart, T. (1997). *Intellectual Capital: The New Wealth of Organizations*. New York: Currency/Doubleday.

Stone, B. and Vance, A. (2009). 'Apple's obsession with secrecy grows stronger'. *New York Times*, 22 June. At www.nytimes.com/2009/06/23/technology/23apple.html?hp&_r=0 (accessed 13 July 2014).

Szulanski, G. (1996). 'Exploring internal stickiness: Impediments to the transfer of best practice within the firm'. *Strategic Management Journal* 17: 27–43.

Taleb, N.N. (2007). *The Black Swan: The Impact of the Highly Improbable*. London: Penguin.

Taylor, F.W. (1911). *The Principles of Scientific Management*. New York: Harper & Brothers.

Telegraph, The (2013). 'NHS boss praised scandal hit hospitals during the height of care debacle, letter shows'. *The Telegraph*, 19 February. At www.telegraph.co.uk/health/healthnews/9879216/NHS-boss-praised-scandal-hit-hospitals-during-the-height-of-care-debacle-letter-shows.html (accessed 13 July 2014).

TreasuryDirect (2014). 'The debt to the penny and who holds it'. At www.treasurydirect.gov/NP/BPDLogin?application=np (accessed 10 July 2014).

Tsang, E.W.K. (2008). 'Transferring knowledge to acquisition joint ventures: An organizational unlearning perspective'. *Management Learning* 39 (1): 5–20.

Turnbull, H.W. (ed.) (1959). *The Correspondence of Isaac Newton*, vol. 1. Cambridge: Cambridge University Press.

United Nations (UN) (2008). *Creative Economy Report 2008: The Challenge of Assessing the Creative Economy: Towards Informed Policy-Making*. New York: United Nations.

United Nations (UN) (2010). *Creative Economy Report 2010: Creative Economy: A Feasible Development Option*. New York: United Nations.

United Nations (UN) (2013). *Creative Economy Report 2013: Widening and Local Development Pathways*. New York: United Nations.

van der Spek, R. and Spijkervet, A. (1997). 'Knowledge management: Dealing intelligently with knowledge'. In J. Liebowitz and L. Wilcox (eds), *Knowledge Management and Its Integrative Elements*, pp. 31–59. Boca Raton, FL: CRC Press.

Vera, D. and Crossan, M. (2005). 'Organizational learning and knowledge management: Towards an integrative framework'. In M. Easterby-Smith and M.A. Lyles (eds), *The Blackwell Handbook of Organizational Learning and Knowledge Management*, pp. 122–41. Oxford: Blackwell.

Vitek, B. and Jackson, W. (eds) (2008). *The Virtues of Ignorance: Complexity, Sustainability, and the Limits of Knowledge*. Lexington, KY: University of Kentucky Press.

von Hayek, F.A. (1945). 'The use of knowledge in society'. *The American Economic Review* 35 (4): 519–30.

von Hippel, E. (1994). 'Sticky information and the locus of problem solving: Implications for innovation'. *Management Science* 40 (4): 429–39.

von Hippel, E. (2005). *Democratizing Innovation.* Cambridge, MA: MIT Press.

Wallace, D.P. (2007). *Knowledge Management: Historical and Cross-disciplinary Themes.* Westport, CT: Libraries Unlimited.

Wenger, E. (1998). *Communities of Practice: Learning, Meaning, and Identity.* Cambridge: Cambridge University Press.

Wenger, E., McDermott, R. and Snyder, W.M. (2002). *Cultivating Communities of Practice: A Guide to Managing Knowledge.* Boston, MA: Harvard Business School Press.

Wernerfelt, B. (1984). 'The resource-based view of the firm'. *Strategic Management Journal* 5 (2): 171–80.

Wheldon, H. (2002) [1960]. 'The BBC *Monitor* interview' (broadcast on 13 March 1960). In M.W. Estrin (ed.), *Orson Welles: Interviews*, pp. 77–95. Lafayette, MI: University of Mississippi Press.

Wiener, N. (1948). *Cybernetics: Or Control and Communication in the Animal and the Machine.* Paris, Hermann & Cie and Cambridge, MA: MIT Press.

Wiig, K.M. (1997). 'Knowledge management: Where did it come from and where will it go?' *Expert Systems with Applications* 13 (1): 1–14.

Wilensky, H.L. (1967). *Organizational Intelligence: Knowledge and Policy in Government and Industry.* New York: Basic Books.

Wilson, T. (2002). 'The nonsense of "knowledge management"'. *Information Research* 8 (1). Paper no. 144. At http://InformationR.net/ir/8-1/paper144.html (accessed 20 July 2014).

World Intellectual Property Organization (2013). *World Intellectual Property Indicators, 2013 Edition.* Geneva: World Intellectual Property Organization. At www.wipo.int/export/sites/www/freepublications/en/intproperty/941/wipo_pub_941_2013.pdf (accessed 28 July 2014).

Wright, G. and Cairns, G. (2011). *Scenario Thinking: Practical Approaches to the Future.* London: Palgrave Macmillan.

Zack, M.H. (1999). 'Managing organizational ignorance'. *Knowledge Directions* 1: 36–49. At http://web.cba.neu.edu/~mzack/articles/orgig/orgig.htm (accessed 13 July 2014).

Zahra, S.A. and George, G. (2002). 'Absorptive capacity: A review, reconceptualization, and extension'. *Academy of Management Review* 27 (2): 185–203.

Appendix

Resources for Studying Knowledge Management

▬▬▬ Recommended reading

Amin, A. and Cohendet, P. (2004). *Architectures of Knowledge: Firms, Capabilities and Communities*. Oxford: Oxford University Press.

Audi, R. (2010). *Epistemology: A Contemporary Introduction to the Theory of Knowledge*, 3rd edn. London: Routledge.

DeFillippi, R.J., Arthur, M.B. and Lindsay, V.J. (2006). *Knowledge at Work: Creative Collaboration in the Global Economy*. Oxford: Wiley Blackwell.

Easterby-Smith, M. and Lyles, M.A. (eds) (2011). *Handbook of Organizational Learning and Knowledge Management*, 2nd edn. Chichester: John Wiley & Sons.

Foray, D. (2006). *The Economics of Knowledge*. Cambridge, MA: MIT Press.

Foss, N.J. (2006). *Strategy, Economic Organization, and the Knowledge Economy: The Coordination of Firms and Resources*. Oxford: Oxford University Press.

Hetherington, S. (2012). *Epistemology: The Key Thinkers*. London: Continuum.

Hislop, D. (2013). *Knowledge Management in Organizations*, 3rd edn. Oxford: Oxford University Press.

Ichijo, K. and Nonaka, I. (eds) (2006). *Knowledge Creation and Management: New Challenges for Managers*. Oxford: Oxford University Press.

O'Dell, C. and Hubert, C. (2011). *The New Edge in Knowledge: How Knowledge Management is Changing the Way We Do Business*. Hoboken, NJ: John Wiley & Sons.

Rooney, D., Hearn, G. and Kastella, T. (eds) (2012). *Handbook on the Knowledge Economy*, Vol. 2. Cheltenham: Edward Elgar.

Rooney, D., Hearn, G. and Ninan, A. (eds) (2005). *Handbook on the Knowledge Economy*. Cheltenham: Edward Elgar.

Tsoukas, H. (2005) *Complex Knowledge: Studies in Organizational Epistemology*. Oxford: Oxford University Press.

Web resources

The following websites provide useful resources for those interested in exploring knowledge management further:

- KMWorld Magazine at www.kmworld.com
- Knowledge Management for Development (KM4dev) at www.km4dev.org
- Gurteen Knowledge Website at www.gurteen.com
- Etienne Wenger and Beverly Trayner's website at wenger-trayner.com/our-services
- CPsquare – The Community of Practice on Communities of Practice: http://cpsquare.org
- David Skyrme Associates Knowledge Management web pages at www.skyrme.com/index.htm
- Sveiby Knowledge associates at www.sveiby.com/index.html
- APQC's Knowledge Base (part of the American Productivity and Quality Centre website) at www.apqc.org/APQC-knowledge-base

All these websites were active on 9 July 2014.

Academic journals

There is a growing number of journals concerned with knowledge management. From a survey of 379 experts together with an analysis of journal citation impact data, Alexander Serenko and Nick Bontis (2013: 317) established a list of the 25 journals in the field of knowledge management and intellectual capital. Here are the top 10 journals, in ranking order:

1. *Journal of Knowledge Management*;
2. *Journal of Intellectual Capital*;
3. *The Learning Organization*;
4. *Knowledge Management Research & Practice*;
5. *Knowledge and Process Management*;
6. *International Journal of Knowledge Management*;
7. *Journal of Information and Knowledge Management*;
8. *Journal of Knowledge Management Practice*;
9. *Electronic Journal of Knowledge Management*;
10. *International Journal of Learning and Intellectual Capital*.

Index